What a Load o' Bowls

What a Load o' Bowls

or I'm All Right Jack!

Don East

STANLEY PAUL

London Sydney Auckland Johannesburg

To Mag
My Skip

Stanley Paul & Co Ltd

An imprint of the Random Century Group

Random Century House, 20 Vauxhall Bridge Road,
London SW1V 2SA

Random Century Australia (Pty) Ltd
20 Alfred Street, Milsons Point, Sydney, NSW 2061

Random Century New Zealand Limited
PO Box 40-086, Glenfield, Auckland 10

Century Hutchinson South Africa (Pty) Ltd
PO Box 337, Bergvlei 2012, South Africa

First published 1987
Reprinted in paperback 1988, 1990, 1991 (twice)

Copyright © Don East 1987

Set in Sabon

Printed by Clays Ltd, St Ives plc

British Library Cataloguing in Publication Data
East, Don
   What a load o' bowls
   1. Bowling on the green – Anecdotes,
   facetiae, satire, etc.
   I. Title
   796.31   GV909

ISBN 0 09 173787 7

Contents

Foreword

'There is more to bowls than the mere playing of the game'
Anon

It is hoped that this little book will serve not only as a helpful guide to the raw recruit, but as a source of spiritual refreshment to the long-serving bowler, who – despite many years of devoted service to this fascinating but exasperating game – is still labouring under the childish delusion that the world is a fair and just place.

Note: All the characters in this book are fictitious.

Should our bowling readers instantly identify every single one of them from within the ranks of their own clubs that is hardly the fault of the author.

Prologue

Having taken guard with leisurely nonchalance, Ralph shouldered his bat; stood back and, with regal composure, surveyed the disposition of the fielders. He knew the importance of the moment only too well. Experience had taught him how essential it was for the incoming batsman to show no sign of apprehension, but to establish by his very demeanour an initial superiority over his opponents.

At this point, readers who have turned impatiently to the front cover to confirm that this is, in fact, a book on bowls, would be well advised to examine their whole mental approach to the game. As new bowlers they will be called upon to listen with rapt attention to a host of rambling anecdotes and detailed reminiscences. Unlimited reserves of patience are called for – and in this respect they have already been found wanting.

However, a slight stumble at this first delicately laid trap should not cause undue concern, providing our unwary beginner takes pains to eradicate this obvious character defect before applying for Club Membership. But to continue ...

Ralph took his time. Then with a cavalier gesture he tugged his ancient 1st XI cap to an even jauntier angle over his greying locks, and prepared to face his first ball.

He saw it clearly. He saw it pitch just short of a length and move in to him. He stepped back and across with text-book precision; weight correctly poised; head over the line of the ball – and played a stylish shot to glide the ball away just backward of square.

Unfortunately, elegant though it was, the stroke bore little relation to the trajectory of the ball, which hummed through the sweeping flourish of the bat and smote him a sickening blow in that region tactfully referred to in polite circles as the 'lower stomach'.

There was a moment of complete stillness. Then, incapable of breathing – either in or out – Ralph sagged to his knees and, with a low moan, crumpled into an untidy ball of wretched humanity.

The bowler spun round, hands on hips, and glowered at the umpire. '*How's that!!!?*' he shrieked.

'Out,' said the umpire, with startling alacrity. He had not, if the truth were told, actually witnessed the incident; his attention having been distracted by the welcome sight of the landlord flinging wide the door of the Pig and Bucket. They were open!

'Out,' he affirmed, stabbing a podgy finger at the sky. 'Leg afore wicket.' It had been a long hot afternoon.

Ralph neither heard the verdict, nor saw the upraised finger of dismissal. He was dimly aware of being dragged to his feet; his head thrust between his knees with that strange blend of genuine concern and bawdy jokes so beloved of cricketers on these occasions.

The umpire, parched and impatient, lumbered upon the scene. 'Can thee walk?' he enquired solicitously.

Ralph eased himself gently towards an upright posture and murmured pathetically that he thought he might be able to manage.

The umpire nodded. 'Good,' he said. 'Then you can walk back to the pavilion – 'cos thee's out.' And with a spiteful snigger he waddled urgently back to his post.

Time has not withered this age-old excerpt from the *Umpire's Bumper Fun Book* and it was, as ever, greeted with the traditional outburst of merriment in which Ralph played less than his full part. He turned and limped painfully away – a disconsolate lonely figure, dragging his bat on the dry tufted grass, long shadowed in the evening sun.

The bursts of laughter and mocking innuendos regarding his advancing years wafted after him on the still air, and the realization came to him quite suddenly that his cricketing days were over.

He had, perhaps, gone on just that one season too many.

'Time to pack it in,' he muttered to himself. 'Hmmph! There must be some other game. . . .'

1
Dress and Equipment

And so it was that some weeks later Ralph paused with his hand on the gate and looked up at the weatherbeaten board which bore, in flaking paint, the legend . . .

He peered furtively through a knot hole in the fence to spy out the land, while he summoned the courage to press the latch.

"Ow do?' said a voice, brusquely.

Ralph turned to face a short, fat, bald gentleman, dapper in appearance and complete with a bristling moustache.

'New member?' The question rapped out, long before Ralph had organized his vocal chords to reply to the first one.

Ralph was mesmerized; pinned by the unblinking stare of steel-grey eyes, magnified to enormous proportions by the thick pebble lenses, and overhung with forbidding bushy brows. 'I er . . . er,' he faltered.

'Digby.' A hand thrust forward with the precision of a guardsman. 'George Digby.'

'Oh, er . . . Ralph Manning. How do you do?'

'Don't hang about then. In you go,' commanded George, pushing open the gate and striding past.

Ralph, gently easing his fingers into mobility from the vigorous handclasp, closed the gate carefully and scuttled after George who was waiting, with just a tinge of impatience, along the path.

'Bowled before?' said George.

'No. I er . . .'

'You'll soon pick it up. Nothing to it.'

'I hope so,' said Ralph. 'I've played a bit of cricket and . . .'

'You stick with me. You'll be all right.'

'Oh, thanks,' said Ralph, falling into step beside him. 'Thanks a lot.'

But his companion was regarding the green with a critical eye. 'One or two bad patches here and there. Could do with a cut, too, by the look of it.'

'Could it?' ventured our hero. 'It looks marvellous to me.'

'Needs a cut,' said George, in a tone which indicated that the discussion was now closed.

'Yes,' said Ralph politely. 'Have you been a member long?'

George halted abruptly. Did he detect a note of intentional insolence? 'Me?' he snorted, fixing Ralph with a baleful glare. 'Good Lord, no. Just joined. First time here. Come along, I'll introduce you to the Secretary.' And turning on his heel, he marched purposefully into the clubhouse.

By the time Ralph had recovered his composure and followed him through the door, George was already shaking hands with the Hon.Sec.

'And this is young Manning,' he announced regally. 'Found him outside – dithering about like a tart at a Christening. New member, you know.'

Ralph's hand was clasped in a warm greeting by the Club Secretary and he was led forward to meet the members. There must have been some twenty or more in the clubhouse at the time, and they stepped forward from all corners – eager to grasp the hands of our initiates, who were about to receive their first lesson.

At this point our novice will do well to take careful note that men bowlers are indefatigable handshakers. They may be seen observing this ritual: on arrival, at the start of the game, after the game and on taking their leave. On departing for holidays – and on return. On birthdays, anniversaries – on winning and on losing. In short, every possible occasion for congratulation or commiseration will be seized upon by the bowler as an opportunity for a comradely handclasp.

The reason for this phenomenon is obscure. Many claim that it reflects the true spirit of the game. Others, perhaps of a more cynical bent, dismiss it as a mere facade designed to conceal the bitterness which rankles beneath the surface – even to the extent of seeking to incapacitate one's adversary.

On this last point, our observant recruit would have noted that, alone among the eager throng that pressed forward with hands outstretched, was one elderly gentleman who took immediate evasive action. Painstaking observation revealed that, on the approach of a fellow bowler, old Tom Pugh would thrust his bowling hand firmly into his trouser pocket and counter swiftly with a dextrous flick of his left – to grasp in a firm but friendly greeting any threatening hand thrust towards him.

It was his proud boast that he had not shaken hands during the bowling season these last nineteen years. Never since that day when, with the Club Championship almost within his grasp, his opponent in the semi-final had bestowed upon him such a crushing handshake that his customary delicacy of touch was utterly ruined and he had been soundly trounced. He has never forgotten. He has certainly never forgiven.

Whatever the historical background, current research has revealed that the average club player will shake hands on 1038.63 occasions during the outdoor season. (Comparative figures for the indoor season are not yet available, but investigations are proceeding.)

It is necessary, therefore, for both new and experienced bowlers to be ever watchful in order to minimize the risk of contracting the dreaded 'Bowler's Hand'.

DIAGNOSIS AND TREATMENT

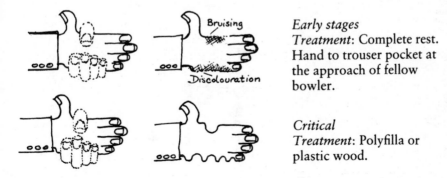

Early stages
Treatment: Complete rest. Hand to trouser pocket at the approach of fellow bowler.

Critical
Treatment: Polyfilla or plastic wood.

When the frenzied greeting ceremony finally subsided the more senior members collapsed weakly into their chairs and the customary awkward silence ensued. Ralph, feeling it incumbent upon him to make some sort of effort, proclaimed with some pride that he had purchased a complete new outfit – including a set of bowls. If he had thought to ingratiate himself with this gesture of unbridled enthusiasm he was soon disillusioned. The sad shakings of heads and the sharp intakes of breath led him to doubt the wisdom of his initiative. 'Right size for you, are they?' said Sid, a dour northcountryman not given to beating about bushes. 'Get 'em out, lad. Let's have a look at 'em.'

Ralph delved into the depths of his brand new real leather hold-all and the gleaming set emerged in all their glory.

'By 'eck!' said Sid, regarding them with some distaste. 'They're little 'uns, ain't they? Nobbut good for a lass is them. Show us your hands, lad. Now, put your fingers like this.'

The studious beginner may already have made acquaintance with the text-book method of calculating the correct size of bowl. The second fingers and thumbs are joined to make a circle (see below). If the tips just meet around the circumference, then the bowl is theoretically the correct size.

Having adjusted Ralph's hands to the required position, Sid placed a bowl upon his outstretched fingers. It slipped straight through, and approximately 3lb of solid plastic, with the consistency of a cannon-ball, landed with a sickening thud on the nail of Ralph's big toe.

Grasping his throbbing foot in one hand, our hero hopped about the clubhouse in a passable imitation of one of the livelier Highland Reels. Sid regarded him thoughtfully. 'There you are,' he said. 'I told you as 'ow they was too little.'

It is inevitable that our new bowler will become involved in this measuring ceremony. But now, forewarned by our Ralph's little misadventure, he will take care to locate a suitable flat surface on which to perform this nonsensical ritual. The time spent is a small price to pay – set against the discomfort of a permanent in-growing toenail.

If he can politely avoid the whole process, so much the better. It does nothing except measure the finger span, which can be done just as well with a small cabbage or a large onion. The problem is not gripping the bowls, but bowling them. Our beginner will find his fellow bowlers only too helpful, and he is advised to borrow from them a variety of sizes and makes. He should try them all out, seek advice and delay buying a set until he is reasonably certain. It is all a matter of personal choice. There is no hard-and-fast method of selection which is generally applicable.

A new set of bowls is an expensive item and until he has gained some experience our beginner is advised to opt for a second-hand set, of which there is a plentiful supply at reasonable prices.

However, similar caution should be exercised towards any such set proffered over-enthusiastically – particularly if accompanied by hints of personal sacrifice or as a special favour. Such phrases as: 'Don't really like to part with them but . . .' should immediately put our newcomer on his guard. Discreet enquiries will often reveal them as an ancient set of straight-running 'four ringers' which have been doing the rounds for years – sold off in turn to every unsuspecting new member. Purchase of the same means that our novice is now saddled with them until the advent of the next gullible recruit.

While Ralph enjoyed a brief period of convalescence, enquiries were made as to the whereabouts of George who, bored with all these technical niceties, had departed to reconnoitre the social amenities of the clubhouse. He was eventually run to earth in the Committee Room, comfortably ensconced in the president's armchair from which he was removed, with some reluctance, and returned to the fold. Whereupon he made it abundantly clear that he had bought nothing. And, what was more, had no intention of doing any such thing until he was told precisely what was required.

The unanimous murmurs of approval which greeted this announce-ment did little to revive Ralph's flagging spirits, but his mortification was far from complete. For it soon emerged that his sparkling new set of bowls was ideally suited to George's pudgy little hands. That fact established, George firmly took possession, overriding our hero's feeble protestations with the magnanimous offer that should they prove to his liking he would, in the fullness of time, be prepared to make a reasonable offer in line with the going rate for discarded second-hand bowls.

George, having no regulation footwear, was then led away by the Hon.Sec. to be fitted out with a pair of overshoes, leaving our hero to ponder on the considerable financial loss already incurred.

These ruminations were cut short by the reappearance of George, now jacketless and displaying over his boldly striped shirt a most eye-catching pair of braces surmounted by a colourful tie which matched neither. Large black overshoes completed the ensemble, which in conjunction with his heavily framed spectacles, created an apparition somewhat reminiscent of a flippered and goggled frogman.

Muted gasps of horror indicated that this regalia fell some way short of the accepted standards of dress. Our beginner will note that most clubs insist on plain white clothing above the waist; with grey or white flannels, depending on the dress of the day – braces, if worn to be invisible.

With regard to the ladies, they are reminded that the rules governing the dress of the lady bowler are laid down by the English Women's Bowling Association, and specify a modestly sleeved white or cream dress or blouse; a white, cream or grey skirt reaching to below the knee, and having two inverted pleats at front and back.

The ensemble is completed by a pair of sturdy flat-soled brown bowling shoes and, on specific occasions, a regulation hat of a pattern bearing the official authorization of the Association.

Accessories are not in order. But, if desired, the effect may be heightened by the permitted single row of plain white beads.

Regrettable as it may be, the stunningly provocative little white number which raised so many eyebrows at the Rugby Club Ball will not, it is feared, pass the scrutiny of the Ladies' Captain.

Restrictive and unimaginative as these rules may appear to the lady novice, she will readily appreciate that they have been framed not only as a safeguard against the wild excesses of an internal fashion contest, but out of thoughtful consideration for her male club mates.

The daring 'off the shoulder' blouse; the risqué plunging neckline and the thigh-revealing split skirt could prove not only a distraction to the serious competitive player, but a positive health hazard to the elderly bowler whose blood pressure is already giving cause for some concern.

While George was being acquainted politely, but firmly, with the rules governing members' dress, Ralph cheered up considerably and permitted himself a slight smirk of smug satisfaction. Not only had he possessed the foresight to don a crisp white shirt; he had also brought along his new white sweater – a fact that had not escaped our frogman's eagle eye.

'Ah,' said George. 'I'll borrow your pullover for today, old man. Not cold, is it?' It was obviously a rhetorical question for George was already rummaging enthusiastically among our hero's possessions. 'Bit on the long side,' he muttered critically, stretching it mercilessly over his ample girth. 'Still, it will do for today.' And wrenching up the dangling sleeves he picked up his newly acquired bowls and made for the door. 'Let's get started then,' he said brusquely, and strode out on to the green.

The Hon.Sec. anxious for the welfare of the sacred turf hastened after him, leaving Ralph to replace the veritable treasure trove of bowling accessories which George had strewn about the floor in his unseemly haste to locate the sweater. The concensus of opinion was that, impressive as they were, most of the extras were unnecessary gimmicks quite superfluous for a beginner, and that in some cases he had been sold the proverbial pup.

When all was cleared away a choice of bowls was produced and, after much discussion, a set was selected for Ralph to try, with the option of a bargain purchase if he liked them. He was then sent off to change.

As he gingerly eased his feet into his new bowling shoes, which pinched his corn and pressed fiercely on his still-throbbing toe, he winced not only at the pain, but at the thought of the money he had wasted on frivolous extras and the wrong set of bowls. If only he had known.

Here again our prospective bowlers are in a fortunate position. They will have made a mental note to buy the best bowling shoes they can afford; to wear them in beforehand; go along to their respective clubs, suitably attired, and rely on the members to give them all the help and advice they will need.

Our hero was now ready. Unfortunately, one slight snag remained. There was no net with his borrowed bowls. Experienced players will be only too aware that the technique of carrying four bowls is far too complex a problem to be dealt with here. It will receive special attention in a later work for advanced students.

Sufficient to say that, after much juggling – and several near misses on his injured toe – Ralph, by the ingenious use of his chin as a third hand, managed to balance them precariously in his arms. With muttered dark threats at the fat little rotter who had pinched his brand new net he hobbled painfully on to the green, where George was ostentatiously studying his watch.

'Oh, do come along, old man,' he said irritably. 'We haven't got all day.'

2
Grip and Delivery

'Right,' said George. 'Now, how shall we play? Tell you what,' he said, with a snap of the fingers, 'I'll take you two on. What about that?'

The Hon.Sec. cleared his throat and suggested diffidently that it might be more helpful if he gave them a few words of advice first. Ralph was most grateful. George frowned; it was not what he had in mind.

'Now the first thing,' said the Hon.Sec., 'is how to hold the bowl.' He prised one from Ralph's nerveless fingers and held it out for them to see. 'This is the grip that I use.'

'Good heavens!' said George, peering critically at the bowl. He turned to Ralph. 'Where on earth did you get these, old man? Bit ancient, aren't they?'

'But,' said the Hon.Sec., hastily forestalling the bitter retort that sprang to Ralph's lips, 'that is only my way. One that I have adopted over the years. This,' he emphasized, turning the bowl in his fingers, 'is in theory the correct, or orthodox grip. Perhaps you would care to try.'

(i) *The Orthodox Grip*

 Technically correct – advocated by most serious text books. Thumb on the large ring; middle finger aligned along the running surface of the bowl. Ensures the bowl will run smoothly on an even keel. But experimentation will reveal that Mother Nature has failed to familiarize herself with these standard works of reference and has, in consequence, designed very few hands that can be contorted to this position without considerable strain.

Having attempted the exercise with little success, Ralph was relieved when the Hon.Sec. invited them to study for a moment the wide variety of individual grips being employed by the other bowlers on the green.

'Not two the same,' said Ralph in mild surprise.

'Quite so,' nodded the Hon.Sec.

(ii) *The Fingertip Grip*

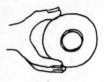

Ensures maximum fingertip sensitivity and enables the middle finger to be aligned as for the Orthodox Grip. Also guarantees that the bowl will instantly slip from the player's numb and nerveless fingers in the biting northeast wind and driving rain which are inseparable from the outdoor season.

(iii) *The Cradle Grip*

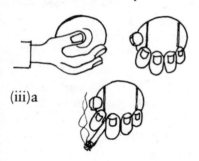

(iii)a

Bowl cradled in the palm of the hand. Some loss of fingertip sensitivity but bowl feels secure, and the fear of dropping it is eliminated.

Also permits heavy smoker to deliver the bowl without the necessity of removing fag from the fingers. See (iii)a.

(iv) *The Hurler's Grip*

Good strong grip. Bowl grasped tightly with all fingers and thumb. Not the remotest possibility of dropping it. Total loss of fingertip control, but useful for banging home a 4in nail.

Bowl liable to perform the most amazing gyrations as it wobbles on its devious course.

(v) *General All-purpose Grip*

A variable grip favoured by most bowlers, combining elements of (i) and (iii) with just a smattering of (ii) – according to the shape and proportion of the individual's hand.

'But the main consideration,' said the Hon.Sec., 'is that the bowl should feel comfortable in the hand, with no sense of strain. Not forgetting,' he added, 'that it is not uncommon for experienced players to vary their grip according to the prevailing conditions and the type of shot they intend to play.'

'Is that so?' said Ralph, fascinated and totally absorbed.

'When are we going to start this game?' demanded George, with some measure of irritation. 'The park closes at sunset, you know.'

The Hon.Sec. carefully adjusted his spectacles to the tip of his nose and, with a stony glance perfected over many years of reluctant schoolmastering, withered our dissenter into submission. 'All in good time, young man,' he said quietly. 'All in good time.'

George scowled; thrust his hands even deeper in his trouser pockets and aimed a spiteful kick at the nearest bowl, forgetting in his pique the sturdiness and solidity of the said object. Ralph was overjoyed. But here our serious student will be well advised to make a mental note that, no matter how intense the provocation, it is foolhardy to vent one's pent-up feelings on the unforgiving bowl.

'And now,' said the Hon.Sec., quite unruffled, 'we come to the actual delivery of the bowl. And, as with the grip, you will find the same divergence of execution.' He invited them once again to observe their fellow bowlers, finally drawing their attention to one particular player. 'Take Eunice for instance,' he suggested.

'Good heavens!' muttered George. Was there no end to this fellow's insensitivity? Was he seriously proposing that a man of George's undoubted ability should look to a mere woman for guidance? It was the final indignity.

'Now there is a delivery you might do worse than copy. Nothing too stylish, mark you, but she gets down well; head still at the moment of delivery, and she keeps it down – gets the bowl away smoothly without bumping it, and follows through with her arm along the line she has selected. What we might call a good steady orthodox action,' he concluded.

Eunice: General all-purpose delivery

Ralph took careful note and nodded his agreement. But his expression soon turned to one of blank bewilderment as his earnest enquiring gaze fell upon the other players as each, in turn, delivered their bowls.

The Plonker

Head well down – pendulum swing. Delivers every bowl exactly the same; regardless of position of the jack. Can be devastating if colleagues are adept at casting the jack to the precise spot which happily coincides with the destination of the Plonker's bowls.

The Flicker

No backswing – bowl is flicked with the fingers. Passionately devoted to long jacks. Often develops from a Plonker who doesn't swing his arm because:

(a) Too old and/or too lazy
(b) Pullover knitted by doting wife has:
  (i) shrunk in the wash
  (ii) never fitted in the first place

The Pitcher

Capable of some remarkable shots. Can draw over opponents' bowls as well as round them. But risky to include in your team as you are liable to be one short when the offender is ordered off the green by irate groundsman.

The Croucher

Not recommended for bowlers suffering from arthritis, tightly fitting trousers or an involuntary tendency to break wind. The last named, whilst not constituting an actual infringement of the Laws, may well be considered prejudicial to the true spirit of the game under the heading of ungentlemanly conduct.

The Stylist

Destination of bowl of secondary importance to style of delivery. Always impressive to onlookers. Bad shots invariably attributed to:

(a) deficiencies of team-mates
(b) irregularities in playing surface
(c) ridiculous instructions from poor skip

Usually hoodwinks selectors – destined for early award of County Badge.

The Wobbler

Can be erratic, but worth his place in any team. The demoralizing effect on the opposition of one shot drawn by the Wobbler is worth any three gained by orthodox deliveries.

Often 'highly critical' with regard to the style and action of other bowlers.

The Gourmet

Preoccupied with direction – not, as it may appear, with eating the bowl.

Compensation for being unable to see the jack is the sheer bliss of obliterating skip from view. Thus hidden, the Gourmet can feign ignorance of skip's frantic signals and select a shot based on personal preference.

Round-arm Slinger

A formidable opponent, against whom there is no known defence, as the unpredictable track of his bowl defies all natural laws of motion.

Faced with such an adversary, the only viable counter plan is total capitulation. Immediate surrender in the face of overwhelming forces beyond the bounds of human understanding.

The Archer

Rarely delivers a short bowl. Can be a very dangerous player – particularly to his own side when they are holding shots.

Holder of firm convictions. Not kindly disposed to accepting advice, instruction – or even abject pleading.

Potential skip.

'Good Lord!' said Ralph, as he completed his inspection. 'Some roll it and some push it.'

'Yes, and some squirt it away with a flick of the fingers,' smiled the Hon.Sec. 'All very puzzling, I know. But remember that it doesn't matter all that much which method you adopt, as long as you do it consistently. That's the thing to aim for – consistency.'

If confirmation was needed he urged them to study the foremost exponents of the game, and to note the same wide range of styles. 'All bowlers,' he continued, 'have some technical fault in their delivery but they automatically compensate for it.' He emphasized that the players they had just been observing were – for all their faults – experienced bowlers who could acquit themselves reasonably well.

George, still smarting from his rebuke, sniffed disparagingly. 'I wasn't all that impressed, I must say,' he said loudly. 'Not your first team, is it?'

He was assured it was not.

'Hmmmmph,' said George. 'Thought not . . . just as well, perhaps,' he smirked.

If the Hon.Sec. was aware of this keen shaft of irony, he gave no sign. 'Well, now you've seen how to do it – and how not,' he added with a smile, 'I think it's time you tried your hand, don't you?'

'Ah,' said George, displaying remarkable agility for his figure. In a trice he had snatched up his bowl and stood four square to the wind, ready in all respects for action. 'Now come along, Ralph,' he said briskly, 'just keep your eye on me, till you get the hang of it.'

3
The Basic Shot – Drawing to the Jack

The Hon.Sec. indicated briefly that the object of the game was to get your bowls nearer to the jack than your opponent's. He showed them how to face the bank and place the mat according to the Laws; and explained that the jack had to be cast a minimum distance of twenty-five yards and then centred.

Thereupon he offered the jack to George, who stepped smartly onto the mat and sent it scudding up the green until, with no apparent decrease in velocity, it disappeared into the ditch at the far end. A short silence followed. The Hon.Sec. cleared his throat and George, sensing the possibility of a mild rebuke, rounded on him: 'Full length, is it, this green of yours? Seems a bit short to me.'

He was assured that it was the maximum length permitted under the Laws of the Game.

'Hmmmmph,' grunted George, indicating that he was far from convinced.

Meanwhile Ralph had scurried off to retrieve the jack and it was agreed that, to save time, he should just place it somewhere – and George was invited to centre it. Basking in this opportunity to display his powers of command, he proceeded to direct the operation with a

repertoire of imperious gestures sufficient to land a crippled bomber on an aircraft carrier wallowing in a Force 10 gale. A procedure punctuated by some outspoken criticism regarding Ralph's pitiful lack of dexterity in carrying out the simplest instructions. 'I don't think the fellow's all that bright, you know,' he observed to all within earshot.

With the jack finally positioned, the Hon.Sec. turned his attention to the bowl and, holding one before him, he indicated the smaller ring which marks the bias.

Small ring   Bias side

'This,' he said, 'is the bias side – and it is in this direction that the bowl will curve.'

'Why?' said George.

With measured deliberation the Hon.Sec. adjusted his spectacles. He did so hope the afternoon was not going to prove tiresome. 'I don't really know,' he said politely.

'Hmmmph,' said George, with thinly veiled contempt, and commenced to whistle tunelessly in a most irritating manner.

The Hon.Sec. pressed on doggedly to explain that if the bowl was held with the bias on the left, it would curl to the left, and vice-versa. Ralph nodded eagerly, anxious to atone for his companion's ungracious conduct.

The Hon.Sec. smiled. 'Good,' he said. 'Now the basic shot of the game is –'

'What's the other side called?' said George bluntly.

The Hon.Sec. regarded him blankly. Good heavens, thought George. Was the fellow trying to be evasive? 'The other side of the bowl,' he said loudly and slowly, as though to a retarded five-year-old with hearing difficulties. 'What's that called?'

A tiny sigh from the Hon.Sec. The afternoon did, in fact, show every sign of being exceedingly tiresome. 'It isn't called anything,' he said quietly. 'Now, as I was saying. The basic shot of the game –'

'Probably called the non-bias side, I should think,' said George. He turned to Ralph. 'Yes, I think you'll find that's the case.'

The Hon.Sec. slowly removed his spectacles and separated his words with deadly precision. 'It – has – no – name,' he enunciated icily. 'The bowl is biased to follow a curving path. I don't know how or why. I have never known. I have no doubt that there is someone, somewhere, who does know. But I do not. And, what is more, I have never had the slightest inclination to delve into the realms of applied science to discover the precise formula. With regard to the opposite side of the bowl,' he continued, choosing his words carefully, 'I should be inclined to dismiss it from your thoughts. Concentrate your mind, if that is at all possible, on the bias mark. If that is on the correct side and travelling along the right course, there is every possibility that the other side of the bowl will accompany it.' And with that he snapped his spectacles back into place and fixed upon our George the cold professional glare which had been honed to perfection on generations of rebellious schoolboys.

Ralph laughed immoderately. From his early days he had been quick to recognize the diplomacy of ready and unstinting appreciation of one's schoolmaster's little witticisms.

George scuffed his feet, but discretion ruled his tongue. He reflected gloomily on the injustice of being saddled with a giggling idiot and a fool of a teacher who, quite obviously, didn't know the first thing about the game.

'Now,' said the Hon.Sec., defying further interruption, 'the basic shot of the game is the "draw" – that is delivering the bowl so that it will come to rest as close as possible to the jack. There is the forehand draw, in which the bowl is directed to the right of the jack from where it will curl in towards it, and vice-versa for the backhand draw.'

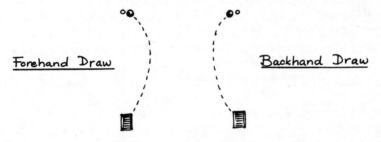

'Remember,' he emphasized, 'to keep the bias mark on the inside. If it is on the outside, you will bowl what is known as a "wrong bias".'

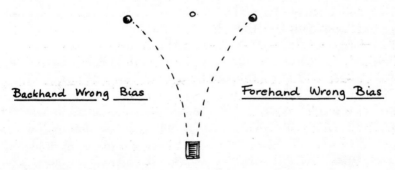

He repeated the instructions with demonstrations to reinforce the points, and enquired whether they were quite clear.

Ralph nodded. 'The same as tennis,' he volunteered.

'Exactly,' beamed the Hon.Sec. Yes indeed, a most apt pupil, and with a keen sense of humour, too.

George, nothing if not resilient, was not to be subdued for long. 'I'm a left-hander,' he announced defiantly.

Perhaps a little unkindly, the Hon.Sec. expressed mild surprise that a man of such talents was not totally ambidextrous, but relented to explain that it made no difference – the terms were merely reversed. 'The wrong bias, however,' he said, looking hard at George, 'is unaffected, and can prove equally disastrous.'

Here our prospective bowler will note the emphasis placed upon the wrong bias. It is easily done, but the consequences – of which more later – may be out of all proportion to the gravity of the offence. Our novice should call to mind the all-important dictum – 'small ring on the inside' – every time that he or she steps upon the mat.

The Hon.Sec. turned to his favourite pupil. 'Would you like to try first, Ralph?' George, who had been poised on the mat for some considerable time, gave way with extremely bad grace as Ralph politely eased him aside.

Once on the mat, our hero tried hard to remember everything he had been told – but it was too much.

'Don't stand square on,' said the Hon.Sec. 'Point your feet along the line you are going to bowl.'

Ralph gave up. Trusting to his instincts – and a generous slice of beginner's luck – he delivered his bowl.

He delivered it very smoothly, with no suggestion of a bump, and it rolled serenely up the green. He watched it as it began to bend, almost imperceptibly at first, then – as it gradually lost pace – to curl majestically in an ever-steepening arc. He watched with deep satisfaction the subtle delicate curve of a dying bowl as it finally came to rest, quite close to the jack.

He was captivated. Like so many before him, utterly and completely captivated from his very first bowl. And the sheer pleasure of watching the graceful elegance of a bowl in motion was a delight that would remain with him for the rest of his bowling days.

'Oh, well bowled,' beamed the Hon.Sec. 'Well bowled indeed.' Ralph grinned sheepishly. 'Beginner's luck,' he murmured, eagerly picking up another bowl.

But George, temperamentally unsuited to the minor role in which he found himself, was already astride the mat. 'My turn, I think,' he said firmly. And, dispensing with the tedious formalities of assessing line and length, he hitched up the dangling sleeve of Ralph's sweater, drew back his arm and launched the bowl.

Although undoubtedly an optical illusion, it appeared, if anything, to gather pace as it sped across the immaculate turf.

The force of the impact catapulted the jack some two feet into the air and deposited it, second bounce, into the ditch at the far end. The momentum of the bowl was, of course, amply sufficient to brush aside such a trivial obstruction, and it thundered on its relentless course to plop into the ditch, right on top of the jack. George puffed out his chest and turned to his companions to receive his just measure of acclamation.

There followed another short silence.

'Er . . . yes,' said the Hon.Sec., scratching his left ear as he searched for the appropriate comment.

'Not bad, eh?' prompted George, not entirely satisfied with the spontaneous warmth of their acclaim.

It was pointed out that, praiseworthy as his effort had been, it was not quite the object of the exercise. 'The idea, you see,' said the Hon.Sec., 'is to get the bowl close to the jack.'

George was highly indignant. 'Can't get much closer than that, can you?'

The Hon.Sec. scratched his other ear. The argument was irrefutable. 'Shall we start again?' he said quietly.

This time George claimed 'first pot' – as he so delightfully expressed it – and he peered short-sightedly after his bowl as it sailed merrily past the jack and came to rest about four yards through and a good yard and a half to one side. 'Bah! Missed it!' he snorted.

'No, no, no. You are bowling *to* it, not *at* it,' he was reminded gently.

Ralph, riding high on his beginner's luck, delivered yet another superb bowl; this time coming to rest right beside the jack, not six inches away. And the Hon.Sec., basking in this vindication of his tuition, was unstinting in his praise.

'Hmmm,' said George, and drew back his arm.

Ralph was still bathed in a warm glow of euphoria at the sheer perfection of his bowl when, with no hint of warning, it was struck fair and square amidships. His heart sank to his boots as it spun away like a wounded bird, and ended up in the next rink but one.

Although partially stunned by the impact, George's bowl teetered on for some distance before stopping just short of the ditch. 'Ah,' said George, drawing himself up to his full 5ft 4in and taking a deep breath. 'Two shots to me, I think.'

'No, no, no!' snapped the Hon.Sec. irritably. (There is a limit to a chap's patience.) 'That's not the way. Not the way at all.'

'Really?' said George. 'Who's winning then?'

Again, as a debating point it was beyond dispute. 'You must try and bowl a length,' pleaded his mentor. 'Draw *to* the jack.'

George was genuinely puzzled. 'What on earth did you think I was doing?'

The Hon.Sec. was a beaten man. He slumped into the nearest deck chair and waved his hand in a limp gesture.

'Carry on,' he said brokenly. 'Carry on.'

But Ralph, too, was a broken reed, his confidence shattered by recent events. He delivered a poor bowl; straight up the middle, so that it curled away from the jack instead of towards it. And he had to confess, when questioned, that he had looked at the jack when delivering the bowl. 'That's the one thing you must never do,' said the Hon.Sec. 'Under no circumstances whatsoever.'

'Why not?' said George, by now thoroughly disgruntled. 'You're bowling at it.'

'*To* it – not *at* it!' yelled the Hon.Sec., and instantly regretted this momentary loss of self-control. 'If you look at the jack, your arm will follow your eye; you will send your bowl on a narrow line and it will curl away.'

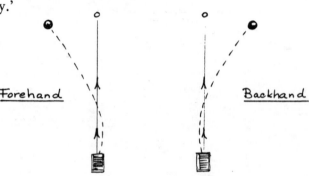

Forehand   Backhand

Looking at the jack

The man's a fool, thought George, but Ralph reflected for a moment. 'Then what exactly do I look at?' he said plaintively.

'Ah,' said the Hon.Sec. 'Ah,' he repeated, 'I was wondering when you would ask. That is, indeed the question.'

'Well, what's the answer?' said George rudely. He felt he was well on the way to mastering this game of bowls, and he did not relish any more long-winded interruptions.

He was quelled with a look, and it was explained to them that some bowlers, having picked out the line, looked up the green to what was termed the 'shoulder' – that is the widest point of the arc; the point at which the bowl starts to curl inwards.

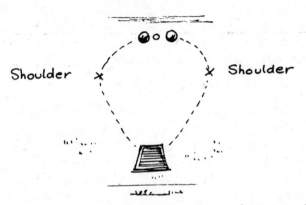

Others preferred to picture an imaginary jack to one side of the actual one, and take this as their guide.

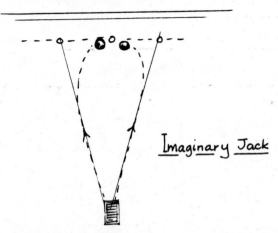

Another alternative, favoured by some players, is to select a mark – real or imaginary – somewhere along the line, and bowl over it.

Yet again, there were many bowlers who visualized the complete track that the bowl would follow, and did not look at any particular point.

The Hon.Sec. confessed that it was, once again, a matter of personal preference and that they would arrive at their own particular method by experiment and practice.

'For instance,' he continued, 'there are those among us who are firm believers in the "fixed object" system. In others words, sighting a line at an object on or beyond the bank.'

Our new bowler is hereby warned that he is liable to encounter the Fixed Object Disciple (or FOD) very early in his career, for the FOD, although harmless and well-intentioned, preys chiefly upon the beginner. But careful study of the following paragraph should enable our student to identify a member of the species, and be on his guard.

The FOD – Behaviour Pattern and Recognition Signals

Having selected a suitable novice, the FOD will sidle up while his victim is waiting his turn to bowl, nudge him gently in the ribs and, in a conspiratorial whisper, hiss barely audible instructions into his ear, e.g., 'Psst! Forehand – gate on the right; third paling along. Backhand – Old Tom's left knee.' And, with a knowing wink, he will melt away into the shadows.

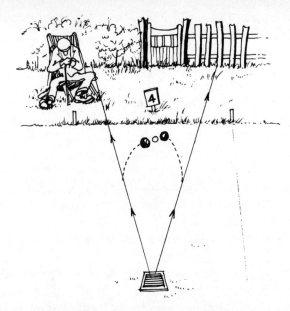

Our novice is urged to treat this advice with extreme caution. Such guiding objects can be ephemeral. When it comes to his turn to bowl he may be distressed to find that Old Tom, who has a tiresome prostate condition, has pottered off to the toilet, and the skip's large lady wife has arrived to drag him home and is concealing not only the paling in question, but half the gate and three parts of the fence.

The Hon.Sec. did not deny that many bowlers had enjoyed considerable success with this method, but urged his pupils to have an alternative plan up their sleeve in case there were no suitable fixed objects in sight. 'For,' he said, and paused for emphasis, 'I must tell you that the Laws of the Game specifically forbid the positioning on the bank of any object which might serve as a guiding mark.'

Our aspiring bowler may be surprised at the necessity for such a rule in a game for gentlefolk. Alas, it must be admitted that, even among the ranks of the fine upstanding bowling fraternity, there exists the occasional black sheep known as the Surreptitiously Positioned Object Disciple – hereinafter referred to as the SPOD.

The SPOD – Behaviour Pattern and Recognition Signals

The species is, fortunately, of a somewhat naive disposition and should present few identification problems, even to our raw recruit.

The SPOD is instantly recognizable as he emerges from the club-house loaded down with spare bags, hold-all, duster, thermos flask, daily newspaper and sundry impedimenta and, despite the sun blazing down from a clear blue sky, draped about with spare sweaters, waterproofs and a thick woollen scarf.

The SPOD going out to bowl

During the trial ends the SPOD will take careful note of the correct lines and surreptitiously position the aforementioned objects on the bank, as guiding marks for the forehand and backhand in both directions.

Should our novice be under the misconception that such question-

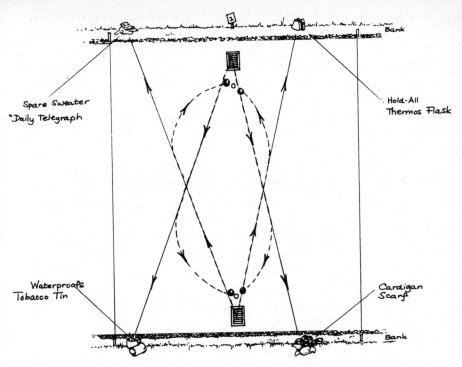

Bank

Spare Sweater
"Daily Telegraph"

Hold-All
Thermos Flask

Waterproofs
Tobacco Tin

Cardigan
Scarf

Bank

SPOD plan – basic lay-out

able tactics are the exclusive preserve of the male bowler, it should be noted that the LADY SPOD – with the extensive range of feminine accessories at her disposal – is in a position to augment the aforementioned list with an exquisite array of tissues, perfumes and toiletries, temporarily transforming the bank into a reasonable facsimile of the perfumery counter in one of the better-class department stores.

These additional items, at which it would be oafish of the true gentleman to protest, not only offer the LADY SPOD the opportunity of bringing a measure of subtle refinement to her game, but render it impossible for her luckless opponent to find a vacant spot for his own little gadgets.

The gentleman bowler, incautious enough to become involved in mixed competitive play, may find himself in an invidious position. On the grounds of olde worlde gallantry, the unfortunate fellow may feel obliged to assist in the transportation of the LADY SPOD's heavy and cumbersome range of visual aids to the bank – thus contributing to his own downfall, and the demeaning experience of yet another sound thrashing at the hands of the demure and gentle sex.

'Like all innovations,' said the Hon.Sec., 'it met with some initial success. Gentlemen bowlers were loathe to resort to direct accusations, which would inevitably lead to nose-to-nose confrontations, and a great deal of unpleasantness all round. But, apart from cheating,' he continued, 'it is not a ploy to be recommended.' In fact, since the introduction of various anti-SPOD measures, such despicable conduct can prove a definite disadvantage against a skilful exponent of such counter measures.

The SPOD Counter-plan

Upon the realization that he is competing against a SPOD, the non-SPOD (or innocent participant) should take immediate steps to keep the guiding objects on the move.

To avoid detection, adjustments should be made only when the SPOD is in the act of delivering his bowl, and the alterations, in the early stages, should be of a fractional and subtle nature.

SPOD counter-plan Note superb technique and timing of the 'Innocent'

As the game progresses, and the efforts of the SPOD to find his line become more frantic, the deviations may be steadily increased.

Towards the end, by which time the SPOD has become totally distraught and practically gibbering with impotent rage, our innocent may throw caution to the wind and rearrange the accessories with reckless abandon.

Special note: There are no contingency plans available, nor are they necessary for a SPOD *v.* SPOD game.

All reports indicate that the banks become so cluttered with assorted bric-à-brac that the combatants merely succeed in confusing themselves. They are best left to their own devices.

'Well, there you are,' said the Hon.Sec. with a smile. 'What do I look at is the question every beginner asks; and they never get the answer they want because there isn't one. . . . The strange thing is,' he mused, 'the better the bowler, the less sure he is about where he is actually looking at the precise moment he delivers his bowl.'

He regarded their blank faces with a sympathetic smile. 'Well, let's try again, shall we?'

Ralph decided, rightly or wrongly, to try looking at the shoulder – and it did not turn out too badly; less than a yard away.

The Hon.Sec. smiled benignly. 'Well done. That's the way; that's all you have to do. Not too much theory – just set it off in the right direction, at the right speed – and the bowl will do the rest.' And having thus summed up the very essence of the game in those few simple words, he rekindled his ancient briar and relaxed, content in the satisfaction of a job well done.

'Pity he didn't say that in the first place,' muttered George, and promptly smashed the jack into the ditch with even greater ferocity than the first time.

The stem of the briar cracked ominously as the Hon.Sec. clenched his teeth. He could stand no more. Only a timely invitation from his pals to make up a triples averted a severe bout of apoplexy. With hasty admonishments on the benefits of diligent practice, he scuttled away to restore his sanity.

'Thank the Lord for that,' said George. 'Too much talk, you know. I've lost my length now.'

Ralph refrained from comment.

'Tell you what,' said George, prodding our hero with a podgy forefinger, 'now you're beginning to get the hang of things, I'll play you for a couple of bob, eh?'

Ralph had been about to suggest a session of individual practice.

'Here you are then,' said George, thrusting a bowl into his reluctant hand. 'Your turn. Off you go. I've got the shot – the jack's in the ditch.'

4
Practice and Theory

Ralph would much have preferred to practice on his own, but his tentative suggestion was summarily dismissed. Here our aspiring bowler should note that there is no real substitute for individual practice: going out on the green with four bowls and two mats to practise the basic shot of the game – the draw. And, certainly to begin with, it is a good plan to leave the jack in the clubhouse. Try to deliver the bowls so that they stop *on* the opposite mat. This will reinforce the idea of drawing *to* a spot, instead of *at* a target.

Drawing practice can become very tedious and if it is regarded merely as a necessary evil it can do more harm than good. To ensure it is an interesting and worthwhile exercise our recruit should bear in mind the following *practice points*:

1. Bowl forehand and backhand alternately to avoid establishing a preference for either. 'One-handed bowlers' are ten a penny – and even at this exchange rate they are grossly overvalued.
2. Constantly vary the length by altering the positions of both mats to avoid developing a preference for long or short jacks. (For 'Long' and 'Short' jack bowlers see 'One-handed bowlers'.)
3. Don't practise for too long. It is physically tiring and after half an hour concentration flags.
4. Don't be tempted to concentrate on what you can't do – it undermines confidence. Keep both hands and all lengths going all the time. When you are pleased with your progress – *stop*. Return again for another session later, but have a break first.
5. When you are satisfied that you have established the idea of bowling *to* a target, start using a jack. Be prepared to resume using only the mats if there is any temptation to bowl *at* the jack.
6. When you can stop all four bowls on the mat, *stop* at once, and write your own book.

Despite the distractions of his playing partner, Ralph persevered and made steady progress. He was beginning to get the idea of length and line, and felt reasonably pleased with himself. George, too, was eminently satisfied. He was striking both jack and bowl – not only with considerable force but with a percentage of direct hits far in excess of the Law of Averages. 'Should have taken this up years ago,' he beamed, pocketing yet another of Ralph's ten-pence pieces. 'Funny thing, you know – one never realizes one's natural talents until one tries.'

In all fairness it must be admitted that this first flush of success was not attributable to his drawing prowess, but to the fact that very few of Ralph's carefully drawn bowls remained on the rink for any length of time. But our hero was not to be deflected from his task and, in the face of this constant bombardment, acquitted himself very well.

So well, in fact, that it did not go unnoticed. Even the players on the next rink, deeply involved as they were in the deadly serious business of the Ladies' Triples Semi-final, took occasion to notice Ralph's efforts. 'Who's the new man?' said Martha. 'I've seen worse.' This, from Martha, was high praise indeed. But their game, at the moment, was too delicately balanced to permit more than a cursory glance. The situation was critical; the result of the match hung on this last vital end.

Was it fate? – Some quirk of destiny, or some cruel jest of the Gods that Ralph should choose this moment to deliver a bowl of sheer perfection, coming to rest against the jack, caressing it with the gentlest of touches.

Ralph could not resist a shy glance towards the Triples players to see if they had noticed. But they were too engrossed. They had not seen it. But George had. He fixed it with a malevolent eye and, moustache bristling with indignation, he snatched up his bowl and drew back that lethal arm.

Straight and true sped the bowl – but, alas, only to begin with. George, in his unseemly haste, had neglected to check the bias mark. Halfway up the green it began to veer away, curling menacingly towards the next rink. 'Look out!' came a despairing cry. But human-reaction time was no match for the speeding bowl as it careered like an avenging torpedo, hell bent on destruction. It hammered into the head. Bowls and jack exploded like shrapnel in all directions, and the three shot bowls which would have clinched a win for Martha's side were dispersed to all parts of the green.

The hideous clatter subsided. A hush hung heavy in the still air – only the distant twitter of a lone sparrow impinged upon the silence. Martha raised her duster aloft for a moment, then hurled it to the ground. '*****!' she said.

The aspiring bowler should note that ungentlemanly, and indeed, unladylike conduct is out of order on the green, except in the most extenuating circumstances. It was unanimously agreed that the afore-mentioned incident constituted justifiable provocation.

Joan, the opposing skip, was unable to contain herself. 'No end!' she cried with great glee, then checked herself. 'Sorry about that, Martha. What bad luck,' she said glumly, hardly able to keep a straight face. 'We shall have to play that end again, I'm afraid.'

This was not strictly correct (as reference to Law 38(c) will confirm). And here our prospective recruit should observe that the greatest single factor shared by the majority of bowlers is a stubborn pride in remaining somewhat hazy about the Laws of the Game. The guiding principle in any dispute is that the bowler who bluffs with the greatest air of authority will usually carry the day.

The Laws meant nothing to Ralph, whose immediate instinct was to take to his heels. His horror turned to amazement as he beheld George striding purposefully up the green towards the scene of the holocaust. Whatever one felt about the little chap, his courage was beyond question. George picked his way through the debris and peered about him. 'I say, my dear,' he said chirpily, 'have you got my bowl among this lot?'

Martha growled menacingly, retrieved her duster with regal dignity and turned her back on him.

Joan was only too happy to find it for him, and while she searched George cast a critical eye at the spreadeagled bowls. 'Not doing too well today, your girls are they?' Joan's mouth fell open. 'Still never mind,' said George. 'I expect you'll soon get them up to the mark.' And with those few words of encouragement he turned on his heel and, whistling a merry military air, he marched briskly back to where Ralph was waiting patiently on the mat. 'If you don't mind,' said George, easing him gently aside, 'I'll just bowl this one again. Damn thing must have been round the wrong way.'

Our heroes continued. The Triples replayed that last fateful end. Martha's side went two shots down, and the match was lost. In less enlightened times it may well have been a matter for a lynching party, but George was quite oblivious to the dark glowerings of Martha and her girls as they trouped disconsolately into the clubhouse. Quite oblivious to the fact that he had carved a niche for himself in the annals of the club on this his very first day.

No excuse is offered for reminding our raw recruit yet again of the time-honoured adage: '*small ring on the inside*'.

*

As the afternoon wore on scudding clouds obscured the sun, and the stiffening breeze, veering north-northeast, flapped the sleeves of Ralph's flimsy shirt and cut clean through his summer vest. 'Getting a bit chilly,' he ventured tentatively. George looked up sharply. 'Chilly?' he snorted. His luck was still holding and the steady influx of Ralph's ten-pence pieces was warming the very cockles of his heart.

'Well er . . . just a little,' murmured Ralph apologetically.

George eyed him from deep in the folds of his companion's thick sweater, in which he was snugly cocooned. 'Feel the cold do you?' he asked disparagingly.

Ralph was about to comment acidly on the gross injustice of the pullover situation, but George had stepped on the mat and promptly brought off yet another three-ball cannon plant worthy of the *Guinness Book of Records*.

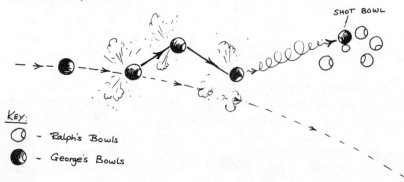

Three-ball cannon plant (George Digby, c.1985)

But it couldn't last. Inevitably he began to miss, and the ten-pence pieces steadily returned to the pocket of their rightful owner. And as they dwindled away; so dwindled George's enthusiasm. 'I think that's enough for me,' he said brusquely. 'Don't want you to catch cold, old man.'

Ralph, in fact, had not noticed the cold since the upturn in his fortunes and was about to demur.

'To tell the truth,' said George, retrieving his bowls from the ditch, 'I'm getting a bit bored with all this. I think we've mastered this drawing business, you know. Need to move on to the tactical side. Now, that's what interests me.' And returning our hero's sweater with a magnanimous gesture, he turned towards the clubhouse. 'I'll go and have a word with Martha and her girls. I thought they looked a bit down in the dumps. See if I can cheer them up.'

Ralph stayed firmly where he was. Domestic disputes on a purely one-to-one basis were troubles enough. He had no intention of becoming involved in a free and frank exchange of views with an irate Ladies' Triple harbouring a justifiable grievance. Alone at last, and relishing the welcome prospect of a spot of serious practice, he gratefully pulled on his sweater. It was not a pretty sight. In his vigorous exertions to mould the garment to his unusual contours, George had effected certain modifications, both in size and style.

Ralph resolved on the instant that his devoted wife, who had knitted laboriously throughout the long winter evenings, must never set eyes on it. If cornered on the subject of bringing it home for washing he would claim that it had been (a) lost (b) borrowed (c) stolen (d) incinerated, depending whether the current mood of the afore-mentioned lady was (a) gullible (b) conciliatory (c) suspicious (d) acid.

*

Left to his own devices our hero, who had a natural aptitude for ball games, made considerable progress. And it was a very happy and contented new bowler who – after due observation of the 'hand-shaking-on-going-home-for-tea' ceremony – whistled his homeward way. He would have liked to stay for tea and play on afterwards but, unaware of the existence of such extended delights, he had not forewarned his good lady.

Special note: Prospective bowlers already ensnared in the joys of wedlock will be relieved to learn that this knotty problem will be allocated ample space in a later work.

Extra special note: No consideration whatsover will be given to existing bowlers who subsequently opt for wedded bliss as:

(a) their number is so small as to be insignificant
(b) They are probably receiving more than their fair share of advice already
(c) They must be very poor bowlers

His enthusiasm fired by his early success, Ralph called in at the library to denude the shelves of every book he could find on the subject of bowls. Thus equipped he toddled off home, where the coolness of his reception was matched only by the temperature of his evening meal. His dear lady held very firm convictions on the subject of meal-time punctuality. And the fact that his preoccupation rendered him oblivious to the somewhat strained atmosphere did little to enhance the situation. With book propped against the milk jug and totally absorbed in the problem of overcoming the forehand wobble, he devoured with apparent relish the congealed haddock and cold stewed tea set before him as a corrective punishment. Not even that familiar warning signal – the rhythmic tapping of a female fingernail on the table top – had its customary chastening effect.

Hardly pausing to swallow the last mouthful our hero, anxious to put all these theories into practice, leaped from his chair to spend the entire evening, book in hand, delivering countless imaginary bowls in the direction of the kitchen door.

Taking each book in turn he strove to follow the advice contained therein, adopting and discarding the different theories of each successive author. Somewhere in these books he was convinced must be the answer to absolute perfection. He was determined to seek it out.

The TV screen, still and grey, stared blankly into space, his favourite programme forgotten. The elderly Labrador, lead in mouth, looked on, whimpering softly, and from time to time casting a soulful glance at his mistress as if seeking reassurance regarding their master's mental state. No such reassurance was forthcoming. She had, in fact, her own very grave doubts on the matter.

Eventually, finding it impossible to elicit more than a vague grunt in response to their overtures, both dog and mistress retired to bed and left him to it.

The following day, brimful of optimistic confidence, Ralph hurried down to the club. But alas – with his brain and limbs befuddled with a host of conflicting theories and methods – he was unable to deliver one good bowl. He bumped them, he wobbled them, even dropped them, and became so distraught that he went from bad to worse.

His distress was absolute. And it was not alleviated by the arrival of George who, complete with a pint of best bitter, ensconced himself in a nearby deck chair and joyfully devoted himself to a comprehensive and scathing criticism of our hero's current form.

It was not in the least helpful and Ralph, suppressing the urge to resort to physical violence, was eventually driven to enquire, with heavy sarcasm, whether his companion himself was contemplating a little practice.

George very nearly spilt his ale. 'Good Lord, no!' he spluttered. 'I did all that yesterday. That was enough for me . . . but you carry on,' he said, with a regal gesture. 'That is, if you feel it's doing you any good.'

Ralph took a deep breath and tried again.

'Rubbish,' said George. If somewhat lacking in constructive encouragement, the comment was not without justification. 'Your trouble,' said George, wiping the froth from his moustache, 'is worrying too much about your end of the business. You want to concentrate more on where the thing is going to *stop* – that's what matters, you know.'

Ralph sniffed disdainfully. But our reader should observe that he would have been wiser to heed this simple piece of advice. Every beginner should bring total concentration to where the bowl is going to *stop* – not how it is going to *start*. An elegant delivery style does not guarantee the bowl will finish anywhere near the jack – bowling a good *length* guarantees it will never be far away. Concentrate on length – delivery style can be perfected later.

Bowling clubs are most considerate to new members and Highcliffe was no exception. Seeing them on their own, they were immediately invited to join the afternoon game which was just starting. Ralph politely declined. He was thoroughly unhappy with the way he was bowling and he could not face the embarrassment. And he had no intention of spoiling the game for the others.

George had no such inhibitions. He was out of his chair like a whippet. 'I don't mind skipping, if you're short,' he volunteered. He had decided right from the start that there was only one job worth the candle in this game of bowls – a position ideally suited to his inborn qualities of command.

Profuse thanks were extended for his thoughtful offer, and he was assured that it would be borne in mind for future occasions. 'Any time,' said George. 'Any time you're stuck, just say the word. Only too happy to oblige.'

Left alone, Ralph tried again. But it was no use. Sadly he replaced his bowls in his locker, and trudged despondently home.

His wife's delight at his early return was soon dimmed by the cloud of gloom which he cast over the house. He picked morosely at his food, then slumped in his armchair and stared in taciturn silence as TV programmes came and went. Not even the highlights of the World Bowls Championships could lift his spirits. In fact, the sight of this galaxy of National Champions, bowling an immaculate line and length and placing their bowls exactly where they were aiming, served only to deepen his dejection.

And then ... he sat forward quickly and peered intently at the screen. The camera had zoomed in for a close up of the action of the author of the very book he had taken as his bible . . . there it was again. He snatched up the discarded book and thumbed frantically through the pages, seeking the illustration he wanted.

The elderly Labrador, startled from his slumbers by this violent eruption, withdrew discreetly to observe developments from behind the kitchen door. He was not one of the bulldog breed.

Could this be true? Could it be that the author was not observing the precise method that he had so meticulously advocated? He was not. He was not contorting his hand to grip the bowl in the manner that Ralph had been striving to copy. Neither was he employing the exaggerated follow-through which was causing our hero such a problem. 'That's not what it says here,' said Ralph indignantly, thrusting the offending illustration within an inch of his beloved's nose. 'Doesn't it, dear,' she said soothingly. 'Oh, what a shame.'

The longer he watched the more he wondered. Could it be true that all these books – with their conflicting theories that he had foolishly tried to combine into one – were attempting the impossible task of defining in words a physical action which was intensely personal and intuitive?

His thoughts went back to his cricketing days, and the words of Don Bradman, arguably the greatest batsman of all time, when asked by a young admirer the secret of how to hold a cricket bat. The youngster was prepared for a long and technical dissertation. The great Don thought for a moment. 'Lean it against a wall,' he said, 'then pick it up as though you are going to chop down the nearest tree – that's your natural grip, son.'

'That's it!' cried Ralph, bestowing a boisterous hug and a smacking kiss on his astonished beloved. 'I see it now.' 'Do you, dear?' she smiled, much relieved. 'Well, that is nice.' 'Come on, Ben,' said Ralph, clapping his hands heartily. 'Time for your walk.'

The wise old Labrador – long-since resigned to the peculiarities of the human race – was not one to question an unexpected turn of the wheel of fortune. With only the minimal rearrangement of a few rugs and one or two ornaments he was soon in attendance, complete with lead and ready for the off.

The front door closed behind them, the dust settled, and with the touch of a button his beloved erased all those ridiculous figures in white trousers, and settled back to enjoy her favourite serial.

Next day, on his way to the club, he returned the books to the library. 'I've finished with these,' he announced triumphantly, banging them down on the counter with such force that the date stamp, ticket tray and the lady librarian were jolted some distance into the air.

She was not pleased. Was there no end to this hooliganism? Had she not only last week had cause to remonstrate with the elderly gentleman who had so far forgotten himself as to hum a brief selection from *The Merry Widow*? What was the world coming to? 'Thank you,' she said icily.

But his buoyant spirits were not to be subdued. Relieved, both physically and mentally of the weight of those books, he nodded and smiled at the row of disapproving faces glowering in his direction, and went on his way with jaunty step.

At the clubhouse he bumped into his mentor and guide, the Hon.Sec., and in response to his enquiries Ralph recounted, in considerable detail, all his trials and tribulations of the previous day.

The Hon.Sec. nodded. 'Hmmmm. . . . You've been reading all the books, I suppose?' he said kindly.

Ralph was quite taken aback. 'How on earth . . .?' he began. The Hon.Sec. smiled. 'They all do it, you know. All the keen ones that is. . . . Never mind. You'll get over it. Give yourself a year at the game, then you can go back to the books.' He wagged his finger in true schoolmaster fashion: 'And,' he said emphatically, 'one book at a time, young man.'

Ralph emptied his mind of all theories, concentrated on his line and above all his length, and gradually began to regain his former standard. Not even the arrival of George could dampen his spirits. 'Still at it?' said George. 'I should have thought you would have got the hang of it by now.'

Ralph shrugged, gave a little grin, and drew another good bowl.

But George was not watching. His eagle eye had spotted a happy little band setting off for a game of triples on the far rink. 'We'll come in,' he called across. 'Make up a fours.'

The lack of spontaneity in their response indicated some slight misgivings on their part. 'Oh, not him again,' muttered Martha, who was never likely to overlook the incident of the wrong bias. But, in the end, good manners prevailed and a warm, if wary, welcome was extended. 'The other fellow's all right,' said Martha. 'It's that little fat man. He never stops yapping.'

'Come along, Ralph,' said George briskly. 'I've got you a game with some friends of mine. We're making up a fours.'

'Oh ... thanks, George,' said Ralph. 'I think I'll be all right today. Bowling a bit better now.'

George reached up to lay a paternal hand on his shoulder. 'Rely on me, old man. I've had some experience of this team play – nothing to it, you know.'

Ralph was elated. 'I'm really looking forward to this,' he said, hurriedly gathering up his bowls. 'The old team spirit. All pulling together for the good of the side. All for one – and one for all.'

George stared at his departing figure in sheer disbelief. Such sentiments had never crossed his mind.

'The boy's a fool,' he muttered.

5
Team Play – The Roll-up

New bowlers will inevitably gain their first experience of team play in that time-honoured favourite of the club bowler – 'the roll-up'. It is a game arising spontaneously on an ad hoc basis played for:

(a) Fun
(b) An extremely modest wager
(c) Delaying the return home in order to dodge such tedious domestic chores as:
   (i) Washing up/Drying up (men bowlers only)
  (ii) Cooking/Cleaning/Sewing
 (iii) Papering the ceiling (lady bowlers only)

All of which are severely detrimental to the dedicated bowler's sensitivity of touch and smooth delivery.

The beauty of the 'roll-up' is that it calls for no tiresome preliminary arrangements regarding time or dress and, unlike organized competitive play, it is entirely free from stress ... that is, once the correct number of players have been assembled.

To our novice, the problem of collecting together some six or eight players may appear to be one of a trivial nature. On the surface this would appear to be so, but he should note that bowlers, as a species, possess an in-built mechanism against any form of organization. It is not a case of wilful sabotage, nor rebellious subversion – more a matter of rampant initiative, coupled with a kindly desire to modify the misguided organizer's ridiculous little plan with one or two ideas of their own.

Therefore it came as no surprise to anyone – except our two heroes – that the contenders for the roll-up, now arriving hot-foot from all parts of the compass, were far in excess of the requisite number.

Ralph was somewhat perplexed, but he was instantly reassured that all was well. It was an indication that the standard procedure had been duly observed – and had gone strictly to plan.

Standard Procedure – Organization of Roll-up

One Hon. member (hereinafter referred to as the Instigator) conceiving the notion of a friendly roll-up, sets the ball rolling by inviting one or two friends to join him. Whilst he is enlisting the remaining players, the original recruits – fearful lest they should not have a full complement – extend invitations to their own particular circle of chums. They, in turn, continue with the good work until such time as the wheel comes full circle, and the Instigator is perturbed to receive several cordial invitations to participate in his own enterprise.

At this point the overall picture begins to blur, and splinter groups start to form. A situation not helped by certain members declaring their allegience to more than one group because they:

(a)   have forgotten who it was who asked them in the first place
(b)   thought it was the same lot
(c)   have learnt from bitter experience that the end result will be the usual shambles and they might as well back the field
(d)   are fed up with the whole miserable business

A swift head count now revealed the totally unmanageable and indivisible number of nineteen prospective players – all happily engaged in mutual recriminations and counter-accusations regarding exactly who was supposed to be playing with whom and at whose door the blame should be laid. Needless to say, George played a full and active part in the debate.

However, after a good deal of milling about, additional recruitment – counterbalanced by the departure of two who thought it was the draw for the raffle, and one who went off in a huff – a solution was eventually found, amicable to all. All that is, except the Instigator, who had chosen an unpropitious moment to absent himself in search of additional recruits. In strict accordance with Clause 3 of Sod's Law (see footnote), the only one left without a game was the member who had mooted the idea in the first place. He, too, went off in a huff.

It was decided, mainly by a formidable lady bowler built on the lines of a battle cruiser of the Home Fleet, that it should be a mixed roll-up. And the Gods, once again in skittish mood, playfully decreed that of the two ladies allocated by pure chance to our heroes' group, one should be none other than Martha. The look of unbridled malevolence that flitted across her countenance at the sight of George's presence gave some indication of her feelings on the matter.

Our chubby hero, who had so far made precious little headway in

Footnote:
Sod's Law There are several variations in the definition of this ancient law, but for all applications to the game of bowls the following versions may be regarded as a general all-purpose guide.

'Having contemplated the very worst thing that could possibly happen – the bowler should henceforth accept it as inevitable.'

or

'Cheer up – things could be worse. So I cheered up – and they got worse.'

Sod (c.700–800BC)

endearing himself to the ladies of Highcliffe, did little to further his cause by a series of distinctly audible comments to the effect that it was a pity they had to be cussed up with these damn women; adding the rider that he only hoped they would be up to standard and not make a mockery of the game.

Martha, the current Ladies' County Singles Champion, noted his observations, and filed them for future reference.

Ralph, for his part, was relieved that the deadlock had been resolved, but his optimistic view that they could now start the game merely revealed his woeful lack of experience. The ticklish problems of picking sides and allocating the playing positions were yet to be overcome.

Coin spinning. This traditional method has long since fallen into disfavour with most clubs because:

(a) mathematical odds against 4 heads/4 tails astronomical. Risk of darkness falling before game starts
(b) gradual elimination by 'odd man out' allows unscrupulous bowler to manipulate coin by sleight of hand (that is to say cheat)
(c) risk of physical injury – coin falling on unprotected head
(d) ten-pence coin once lost down drain

Bowlers spinning for sides

Other alternatives, based on scientific methods, share the same disadvantage. That is, any positive result will be instantly nullified by a vociferous minority protesting at the unfair balance of the sides.

After a couple of abortive attempts at this coin-spinning nonsense,

Bowler cheating with coin

purely for the sake of appearances, it was decided unanimously to resort to the customary method of general consensus. And our heroes were privileged to witness the workings of a truly democratic process which, nevertheless, paid due respect to the niceties of seniority and the established pecking order.

Stage I – Selection of Skips: by mutual consent; based on overall bowling ability – subject to certain modifying constraints, e.g.

(a) founder member
(b) looks after club mower
(c) wife prepares match teas
(d) only one with a stick of chalk
(e) heavy bowler – can't draw, etc., etc.

Horace (a) and Sid (c) were duly elected. Our heroes, as beginners, were allocated one to each side and, after a certain amount of subtle bickering, an equable distribution of talent was agreed. So far, so good.

Ralph's drawing ability had been noted and, coupled with the fact that no one else wanted the exacting task, he was nominated to lead for his side. Daisy Plinckton, his opposing No. 1, was a frail elderly lady, but our hero's first inclinations of sympathetic consideration were short-lived.

Ralph did not merely lose the toss – in truth he scarcely caught a glimpse of the coin before his arthritic opponent pounced with the agility of a young tigress to snatch it up almost before it touched the ground. 'Ah. Heads it is,' she beamed, and pocketed it in one deft movement. 'Our jack, Horace.'

Horace stepped purposefully forward. And here our aspiring bowler will observe the emphasis placed by the thoughtful skip on the length of the jack. Remembering that his lead had a tendency to bowl short, Horace took up his position and called for a short medium cast.

Skip indicating required position of jack

Having stepped back some four to five yards to centre the jack, Horace sighed with martyred resignation at the sight of his lead's first bowl coming to rest precisely where he had been standing. He offered a mild rebuke to this effect, but his No. 1, ignoring the all-important precept of 'watching your bowl until it stops', was already rummaging about in search of her next bowl. A common fault which the novice should avoid.

Experienced player studying bowl until it stops

Ralph delivered a creditable bowl within a yard of the jack. His opponent, determined to make amends for being short, promptly despatched her second effort some three yards through. 'That'll come in handy,' she confided in our hero, with a sly nudge. 'Never wasted back there, you know.' Ralph nodded politely, but a puzzled frown flitted across his brow.

Our reader can indeed consider himself a fortunate fellow in that he may spare himself similar confusion by referring to the phrase set down in the Foreword, 'There is more to bowls than the mere playing of the game', and by noting that the spoken word is of equal importance to the well-delivered bowl. Armed with this philosophy, he is well on the way to mastering the governing principles of team play.

First maxim: 'All bad bowls have a subtle and cleverly disguised purpose which may not be readily apparent, until transformed into a valuable contribution by the addition of the appropriate comment.'
Note: All such comments must be made without hesitancy, and in a tone of quiet, calm authority.

Bad Bowls: *Appropriate Comment Checklist*

(Our novice should observe that this is merely a basic list of elementary examples. As he gains experience he will, no doubt, wish to extend his repertoire by introducing subtle nuances and variations of his own.)

Bad bowl	*Appropriate comment*
Three to four yards through	That'll come in handy
	Must have something at the back
	That'll stop them firing
	Nothing for being short
	No good putting them all round the jack
	He'll be pleased with that
	Needed one there
Three to four yards short	That'll come in handy
	That'll stop them firing
	They won't get round that
	That'll give him the line
	That's ready to be knocked up
	That's finished them on that hand
Two yards wide	That'll come in handy
	Didn't want to give them a shoulder
	That's a good guide
	He can use that
	That's where the jack's going
In the ditch	Better there than short
	That's not in his way
	That shows him the pace
	That's given him a line

Bowler delivering appropriate comment

Observe how the experienced bowler – in direct contravention of the Laws of the Game – cleverly retains possession of the mat whilst delivering his oration. This not only ensures the group's undivided attention, but cunningly destroys the concentration of his opponent who is anxiously awaiting his turn to bowl.

Deliveries which are so unspeakably bad as to be beyond even the generous tolerances of the first maxim need not give rise to utter despair. They can be accommodated, by the adept exponent, under the heading of the second maxim: 'No bad bowl is ever the responsibility of the delivering player, but is, at all times, directly attributable to outside influences above and beyond the control of the said player,' e.g.

(a) defect in green (run, slope, bump or worm cast)
(b) wind (gusting, dropping, veering, absence of)
(c) sudden twinge of pain in knee, wrist, hip, lower bowel, etc.
(d) fool of a skip
(e) someone coughed

Explanation procedure is identical to first maxim, but with extra emphasis on retaining possession of the mat.

Further examples of both maxims will be included in this and subsequent chapters, at the end of which our aspiring bowlers are advised to test their aptitude for team play by listing the examples they have memorized.

Team Play – Aptitude Test

Score:	0–10	Fail. Further study necessary
	10–20	Average club standard
	20–30	County standard
	Over 30	Middleton Cup/Johns Trophy

Ralph drew another shot; and now it was George's turn. His drawing ability had been carefully noted and, as a result, he had been instantly demoted to No. 2.

Demoted is a subjective term, for at the top level No. 2 is regarded as a key position. There is more than a grain of truth in the saying that 'a rink is as good as its No. 2'. But at club level it is a place to hide the 'rabbit' – a position bearing something akin to a social stigma.

George, however, was blissfully unaware of this and, regarding it as a step towards the coveted position of skip, he adopted a somewhat condescending attitude to his fellow novice. 'Leading are you, old man,' he smirked. 'No. 2 myself – obviously spotted the old potential.'

And, ignoring the meticulous signals of his skip, he launched his bowl which scudded merrily between Ralph's woods, to nestle beside his No. 1's back bowl.

Skip urgently indicating preference for the opposite hand

'Wrong hand,' said Martha, who – to our hero's chagrin – had managed to usurp the position of No. 3 from under his very nose.

'I beg your pardon, madam,' he bristled.

She regarded him coolly. 'You must follow our skip's instructions. He was indicating the forehand.'

'Didn't see it that way myself,' said George airily. 'I'm better on my backhand, you know.'

Martha peered at the distant speck of George's bowl. 'Really. You do surprise me,' she observed with cutting acidity.

During this brief tactical discussion, George's opposite number had drawn a little short. Short that was until our hero – oblivious to his skip's frantic signals that the situation had now altered – changed to his forehand, and clipped it neatly on to the jack.

'Pah!' snorted George. He spun round to address his fellow players. 'There you are, you see. Now look what he's made me do.'

For a beginner, his instinctive grasp of the maxims was most commendable.

By the time the No. 3s came to bowl, Sid was lying four shots – and a note of rising panic was apparent in the pleadings of both skips. Horace, for a saving bowl somewhere in the head, Sid, for a back bowl in case the jack was knocked through.

Anxious skips pleading for positional bowls

Try as they might, neither of the No. 3s was able to oblige. Sid's man drew two more delightful shots, but was sufficiently adroit to justify his failure with the telling phrase: 'Got to pile them in while we've got the chance – they can't knock them all out.' Ralph scratched his head and pondered on this. He had not quite got the hang of things yet.

Horace ground his teeth just a little as Martha trundled past the head on both occasions, further augmenting their tally of back bowls. 'We've got enough there,' he growled – but his No. 3 was unabashed.

'Got to be up when the shot's against,' she declaimed firmly, to one and all. 'Give the skip a chance.'

Ralph noted the nodding heads and general murmurs of assent, and he began to see a glimmer of daylight.

Having completed their contribution, they set off for the head, passing their skips on the way. Ralph was intrigued to observe the formalities of this 'crossover' manoeuvre, and noted once again the importance of the spoken word in the subtleties of team play.

The Crossover
Positional Play

Whichever team has bowled better shall instantly claim ascendency; assume possession of the rink and march proudly down the centre to receive the plaudits of their skip. The jocularity and general bonhomie is in direct contrast to that of their failed opponents who, in single file, slink furtively along the extremity of the rink, keeping the maximum distance from their disgruntled skip. Averted heads and careful study of the surrounding turf ensures that eye contact is kept to a minimum.

The Crossover – disposition of opposing teams

The Spoken Word

Sid was quick to stifle the general euphoria of his team with the cautionary admonition that they had failed to deliver a back bowl and, consequently, the situation was fraught with danger. It was the mark of an experienced skip in the ascendant position – at once sowing the seeds of blame, and exonerating himself from total responsibility should he fail to hold on to their shots.

Not to be outwitted, his team were equally quick to pour scorn on his undue pessimism, to emphasize that they had done their job, and to indicate that all he had to do with the two bowls at his disposal was to pair up all the opponents' bowls; get the best back and put a blocker in both hands.

The verbal exchanges of Horace's team, conducted as they were from opposite sides of the rink, were in a lower key and of a more taciturn nature.

'Six down – nothing in the head,' growled Horace, apparently addressing the observation to a vacant deck chair on the bank.

His No. 3 dismissed the remark with the brusque rejoinder that the shot was still drawable. 'Plenty to rest on,' said Martha curtly. 'You can't go through.'

George was more positive in his approach. 'Good position at the back, you know. Hit the jack through and we'll have six.'

Provoked to a stinging retort, Horace opened his mouth to reply, but his crushing riposte was pre-empted by the superb timing of his elderly lead. 'Are we holding?' enquired Daisy brusquely, and pottered on her way, leaving her skip with mouth ajar.

Skips and players had now consolidated their respective standpoints, and had firmly established that – whatever disaster might befall – there was no way that they could be held personally responsible. On that note the crossover procedure was deemed to be concluded.

Horace's first bowl, immaculate in line and length, looked certain to save, if not draw the shot. Unfortunately, it failed to scrape past his lead's first short bowl, caught it a glancing blow and was deflected harmlessly to one side.

'Oh, for heaven's sake, man,' growled his elderly lead. 'Do take the green.'

'You're not here,' snarled his No. 3. 'Do be up, man.'

George snorted with disgust. 'Pathetic,' he observed.

Sid, determined to match up the menacing back bowls, was a textbook example of total concentration as he drew back his arm. A hush fell.

'Nothing at the back, you know,' bellowed his No. 3. 'Get something behind.'

Startled by this ill-timed yelp, Sid's smooth swing gave a convulsive jerk, dragging his arm across his body to send the bowl on far too narrow a line. Under the aforementioned Sod's Law, it too collided with the same short bowl, and bundled it into the head.

Groans of dismay mingled with gleeful cheers.

'What on earth are you playing?' snarled his No. 3 in scathing condemnation. 'You've knocked 'em for second.'

The elderly lead, adroit exponent of the first maxim was quick to capitalize on the situation. 'There you are,' said Daisy, proudly indicating her erstwhile short bowl. 'I told you that would come in handy.'

As they now held second bowl, Horace was urged to draw another lest it be removed. 'But be careful,' warned his No. 3, indicating a gentle draw on the backhand.

George, losing patience at this shilly-shallying and over-timid approach, pushed forward to announce a definite preference for a good swift bowl on the forehand. 'We've got all the backs, you know,' he cried in ringing tones. 'Chance to get a few here.'

'If you don't mind,' said Martha, tapping him on the shoulder. 'I'm in charge of the head, you know.'

George sniffed. 'Really,' he said. 'And where may I ask, has it got us? I've got a couple of bob on this, you know.'

Martha placed a bony forefinger on our hero's second shirt button. 'The function of the one's and two's,' she said icily, 'is to *be* up and *shut* up. And in your case, to keep a neat and tidy score card. And now, if you don't mind. . . . This hand, Horace – just a draw.'

It is unlikely that our reader can lay claim to George's highly developed powers of resilience and, to avoid similar humiliation, he is advised that the authority of the No. 3 is a zealously guarded possession. The new bowler is urged to suppress his more imaginative and revolutionary theories during his apprenticeship.

Horace, obeying instructions, drew an excellent bowl – inch perfect. It rested against their second bowl with the gentlest of touches, but unfortunately it was just enough to topple it over so that it was now third. It was sheer bad luck, but his team – who collectively had failed to get a bowl within three yards of the jack – were unanimous in their condemnation.

'Dear, dear, dear,' tutted his No. 3, hurling her duster to the ground. 'He's not the bowler he was, you know.'

'Hmmmmph!' said George triumphantly, his fast-bowl theory thoroughly vindicated.

The elderly lead turned away in disgust. 'What's the good of putting them in the head. He only knocks them out.'

Sid had the last bowl. 'Holding two now,' cried his No. 3. And then – greed overcoming his discretion – he urged his skip to rest out the enemy's two bowls for a grand total of seven shots. Sid did just that. But it was inevitable, as the bowls lay, that he must pick up the jack and run it towards their opponent's back bowls.

'Now look what he's done,' wailed the No. 3. He glared at Sid. 'Only got one now.'

'The man's a buffoon,' muttered George.

Ralph scratched his nose thoughtfully.

As the bowls were kicked back a brief post-mortem was held, and Ralph was pleasantly surprised to ascertain from the general concensus of opinion that they had all bowled pretty well. Only the skips had been found wanting. Both teams were unanimous in the view that their respective skips had let them down rather badly, and their suitability for their exalted positions was much in question.

Pondering deeply on this matter, it took Ralph some little while to realize that it was he alone who was kicking back all the bowls. Generous soul that he was, he dismissed it as pure coincidence that all his colleagues should become immersed in some alternative task at the very moment kicking time arrived.

Our novice is forewarned, particularly if alone in experienced company, to be on his guard to recognize the devious ploys of the:

Bowl-kicking Procedure
On Completion of the End

The No. 1 makes much play of retrieving and cleaning the jack; then fussing meticulously with the placing of the mat. If it is not his jack then so much the better. He can extend his role by presenting same to his opponent with exaggerated olde worlde courtesy – to the point of lightly polishing his opponent's bowl before handing it over with due ceremony.

Experienced No. 2s feel a sudden impulse to fill in the score card in their neatest copper plate; carefully double check the running totals, and fumble endlessly with the numbers on the scoreboard.

No. 3s – usually experienced campaigners and senior members – become deeply engrossed in a serious appraisal of the tactics of the previous end and/or pressing committee matters, such as the possible addition of sliced cucumber to the match teas.

The novice – kicks back the bowls.

Aptitude Test No. 1: Can you identify the novice?

Counter Ploys (Novices – for the use of)

(a) *If Playing No. 1* Make sure you are first to gain possession of the mat. Body checking and fair shoulder charging is permissible, but tripping or trampling geriatric bowlers underfoot is frowned upon in most clubs.

(b) *If Playing No. 2* Make a complete hash of the score card. Liberal scratchings out and faulty arithmetic will ensure long conferences with your opposite number to sort out the mess. In emergency – knock over scoreboard.

(c) *If Playing No. 3.*   Forget it. You have no chance.

Beginners failing to master these counter-measures run the risk of contracting the dreaded 'Novice's Foot', a disability equally as grave and debilitating as 'Bowler's Hand' (see p. 13).

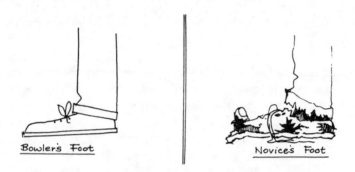

Bowler's Foot   Novice's Foot

The novice foolish enough to disregard these warnings may find his bowling career prematurely curtailed by the dual afflictions of both hand and foot. Not for him the dizzy heights of discussing the merits of the cucumber sandwich – he will be in the kitchen cutting them.

Special note: 'Artful Dodgers'. Fellow members openly bragging about the number of years they have been using the same pair of bowling shoes should be the object of close scrutiny at the conclusion of every end.

When Ralph, hot of foot and perspiring freely, had collected the bowls, jack and mat, the game was able to proceed. Fortunes ebbed and flowed and, although the standard of bowling was not particularly brilliant, the verbal exchanges and the skilful use of both first and second maxims transformed it into a most delightful game to listen to.

Ralph, always a keen student, was most attentive, and among the copious mental notes that he made were a couple which are well worthy of our readers' consideration.

(a) a bowl, for historical reasons, is often referred to as a 'wood' and . . .

(b) never to offer even the most casual enquiry regarding a fellow bowler's state of health. Our hero had committed this minor indiscretion, and the subsequent case history had lasted throughout the next four ends and had embraced: the early symptoms; the diagnosis; a most explicit and gory episode in the operating theatre; the protracted convalescence – rounded off with a detailed summary of some rather indelicate and highly personal side effects.

Our hero, who had been known to blanch at the prospect of a rare cut of beef, felt decidedly queasy. His bowling went to pieces; and only by utilizing the excuse of a chill breeze was he able to decline an enthusiastic invitation to inspect the extensive scar tissue.

Bowler exhibiting operation scar

Horace, by now totally disenchanted with our George's play and attitude, had resorted to the traditional skip's ploy of sniping at his own side by bestowing fulsome praise on their opponents. He singled out Ralph in particular. 'Well bowled, young man,' he enthused. 'You're learning quickly.' He placed a fatherly hand on his shoulder. 'And always make a point of learning something every time you play. No matter who you are, or how long you've played,' he continued, 'there's always something new to learn.' And with a baleful glare at our George he went on his way – little realizing the prophetic truth of his words.

It was on the last end. Horace, for once, was holding two shots and – unable to face the prospect of their removal by yet another of our fat friend's heavy and narrow bowls – he stepped impatiently to the side of the jack. 'You must take your green,' he snapped. 'Look – this is the line. Bowl to my foot.'

George could hardly believe his ears. Such an invitation, and the prospect of a definite target was beyond his wildest dreams.

Only a remarkable display of agility, and a sprightliness of foot which belied his age, enabled Horace to reduce the full force of the impact to a mere glancing blow. It was, however, sufficient to prevent him from taking a full part in the general mirth. As he hobbled round and round in circles, stamping his foot to ease the searing pain of his enraged corn, his fellow skip regarded him thoughtfully.

'As you say, Horace,' he chuckled somewhat tactlessly, 'you learn something new every day.'

Meanwhile, back at the mat, and retaining possession with all the panache of a seasoned professional, George turned to his confederates with a smirk of satisfaction. 'Well the line was right. Spot on, I should say.'

And so the game drew to a close. The obligatory handshaking was observed, and coin of the realm exchanged.

'It's the only way to learn, young man,' said Daisy, smartly pocketing Ralph's twenty pence. 'Always learn by paying out, you know. Er, same time tomorrow?' she enquired breezily, eager to nurture an association which held every promise of a steady, if modest income.

Back in the dressing room Ralph reflected on all that he had learned from his first experience of team play, and while he was thus musing the Hon.Sec. sat down beside him. 'Enjoy your roll-up?' he asked.

Ralph assured him that he had. Very much.

'Good,' said the Hon.Sec. and chuckled softly. 'I see you got in with the old campaigners today. Taught you a thing or two, didn't it?'

Our hero confessed that he had been rather taken aback at the measure of disagreement and the level of mutual recrimination. 'Not quite what I expected,' he had to admit.

The Hon.Sec. chuckled again. 'Never mind what your books tell you,' he said, patting our novice on the shoulder. 'You just remember – a rink is a team of four players, consisting of three skips and a bloody fool.'

6

The Club Match

Ladies' and gents' inter-club matches, although invariably played on a single-sex basis, are identical in every aspect, and it is intended that these cautionary notes – embracing the protocol and mystiques of these harmless little jousts – will prove equally helpful and instructive to both male and female novice.

So great is the similarity that, to avoid tedious and unnecessary duplication, it has been decided to concentrate on a Gents *v.* Gents match. But on no account should this be regarded as an affront to the ladies; nor indeed as a slight upon their undoubted match prowess, which, in every department, is at least equal – if not superior – to that of their male clubmates.

In particular, their natural aptitude for the 'spoken word' – bestowed upon them throughout the ages by a doting Mother Nature – affords them a mastery of this sphere of influence which has long been the envy and admiration of their menfolk.

Parkview BC v. Highcliffe BC

It was but a few days later that our two heroes were approached by the Captain and the Match Secretary with an invitation to play for the Club in a friendly match on the following Saturday. Ralph was flattered at this unexpected honour, but George was of the opinion that this recognition was long overdue – he had been a member now for the best part of a fortnight.

If either had taken the trouble to look at the pitiful lack of names on the Availability List they would have seen that they were far out in their assessment of the situation which – in short – was one of total apathy towards this particular fixture.

The popular demand for a full Match Programme, expressed with such vehemence throughout the long winter and carried with acclamation at the AGM had, as usual, mysteriously evaporated with the onset of the season, leaving the luckless Captain and Match Sec. to beg, bully or cajole the more gullible members into fulfilling the commitment.

Bowler being invited to put his name down for Club Match

Our new bowler should be wary of a flatteringly premature invitation to represent the club, possibly concealing an ulterior motive, i.e. unpopular fixture; no one else wants to go.

To this end club bowlers have at their fingertips an extensive repertoire of unimpeachable reasons for being unable to play, and our novice is urged to commit a selection to memory against any contingency. It is important that they are offered to the Captain or Match Sec. with due solemnity and expressions of acute disappointment. An element of truth is desirable, but by no means essential.

Club Match Excuse List

(a) Spouse – going out/stopping in; ill; much better; in one of those moods

Note: The explanatory details given above are optional. The simple statement in (b) will suffice.

(b) Spouse – has one
(c) Disapproves of: green; bar prices; dressing room; raffle prizes; raspberry jam (pips got under plate on last visit)
(d) Physically unfit – ancient medical certificate kept in wallet clinches the argument
(e) Rained heavily when played there the year before last
(f) Wax in ear – sudden affliction of instant deafness renders pleadings of Match Sec. totally inaudible.

Bowler suffering from Dodgertalius Auralius (Dodger's Earhole)

Novices are warned to beware of despicable Match Sec.'s cunning ruse to undermine your excuse by whispered invitation to have a drink.

Our heroes, in their innocence, had been incautious enough to confess to the ownership of a motor car, and the addition of their names to the list rekindled the enthusiasm of those unfortunate members who suffered from that acute form of travel sickness which – strange to relate – manifests itself only on public transport.

This rapid increase in the number of names did not escape George's beady eyes. He drew Ralph to one side. 'No point in taking both cars, old man,' he said kindly, patting him on the shoulder.

Ralph was about to thank him profusely for his thoughtful offer, but he was cut short.

'I'll come in yours,' said George, and departed.

By the eve of match day George had extended ingratiating invitations to their skip and No. 3, and was thus able to furnish Ralph with: a full complement of passengers; a detailed route map and his itinerary for the day – complete with arrival and departure times.

'Come for me – say 1.30,' he said. 'I'll map-read for you. Done a bit of rallying in my time, you know.'

On the dot of 1.30 Ralph was there. At 1.40 he was still there and his anxiety was mounting when the door was wrenched open. 'Plenty of petrol?' demanded George, plomping into the seat and slamming the door with a sickening jolt that all but stalled the engine. 'Put my bag in the boot will you, old chap? Can't open the damn thing.'

As they passed Ralph's unpretentious little semi-detached, his

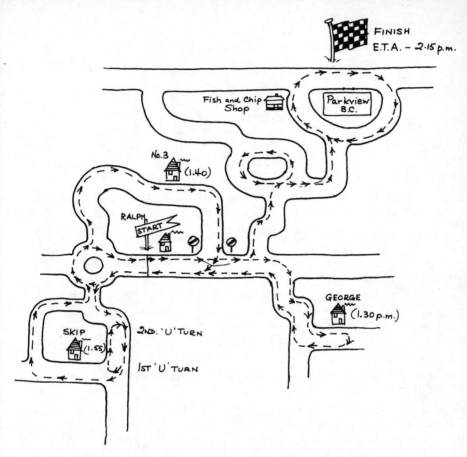

Bowler driver's route map and itinerary (not to scale)

passenger paused in the act of lighting a vicious-looking cigar, to observe that the colour scheme of the paintwork was not one that he, personally, would have chosen. 'Roundabout dead ahead,' he added, stubbing a podgy forefinger on the windscreen. 'Third exit at 3 o'clock. . . . Keep it up. You're doing splendidly.'

Their No. 3 was ready and waiting at his gate, and managed the boot lid reasonably well. The jagged scratch on the paintwork would be but a moment's work with a small can of touch-up spray, readily obtainable from all good motor shops.

The fact that George had pushed back his seat to its farthest extent made access to the rear somewhat hazardous for a bowler long past his athletic prime. But, after much scuffing of carpet and upholstery, No. 3 solved the problem by stumbling head first through the doorway to land face down on the back seat.

However, by the time they were passing Ralph's house for the second time, he had managed to achieve an upright posture and was in a position to concur heartily with George's views on the paintwork – and furthermore, to draw their attention to the very poor condition of the mortar in the garden wall.

It was indeed fortunate that George was able to attract the attention of their skip, as they passed him striding purposefully at a cracking pace in the opposite direction. Herbert, a stickler for punctuality, had set off to meet them. A U-turn was called for. Despite the benefit of George's assistance, our hero executed a hazardous and breathtaking manoeuvre in the face of heavy traffic, only to re-pass his elusive passenger who had spun round and set off in frantic pursuit. But eventually, a combination of frantic gesticulations, wild cries and the squeal of protesting tyres brought about a successful rendezvous; to a smattering of applause and a muted cry of 'Bravo' from a handful of appreciative onlookers, under the misapprehension that a dastardly criminal had been run to earth.

Herbert, by this time wheezing heavily and decidedly fractious, stubbornly refused to be parted from his large bowls bag, which was thrust through the back door – cuffing Ralph smartly on the ear before descending abruptly onto the groin of the No. 3 – who fell strangely silent.

Close behind the bag followed a fearsome briar pipe, clenched between Herbert's teeth and emitting – as a result of his strenuous exertions – a spectacular cascade of sparks and glowing embers which imparted an added texture to the upholstery. Finally ensconced behind his enormous bag, which he had grudgingly removed from his colleague's lap, Herbert was unable to close the door. Only a dare-devil escapade by the owner-driver prevented a passing juggernaut slicing it off at the hinge.

'You prefer a smallish car, do you?' said George deprecatingly, as Ralph, white-faced and visibly shaken, resumed his seat. 'Economical I suppose, but er. . . . Oh, do try and get a move on, old boy,' he urged, thrusting his watch beneath our hero's nose and rapping it loudly with his fingernail. 'Well behind the clock, you know.'

Now at full complement our merry little band set off at a jaunty 19 m.p.h. It was not that the car was unable to cope with the load; but that the formidable combination of pipe and cigar rendered it somewhat difficult to locate the windscreen – let alone see through it.

A non-smoker himself, Ralph made so bold as to lower his window a chink, but the cries of rage from the back regarding the insufferable draught persuaded him to reverse the process, only just in time to allay the fears of a Pakistani newsagent who was on the point of summoning the fire brigade.

If our hero was able to draw any consolation, it was from the fact that, when passing his residence yet once again, poor visibility effectively stifled further adverse comment regarding the dilapidated condition of the property.

George, with map on lap, barked spasmodic commands, but his concentration was centred mainly on expounding the tactical plan he felt they should pursue in the forthcoming match. The No. 3, still preoccupied with his own personal problems, and doubting whether he would ever walk again – let alone bowl – whimpered softly in the corner. Herbert, who hadn't wanted to play in the first place, was totally disinterested and devoted his attention to dotting out his pipe all over the carpet and re-stoking the infernal contraption, while our hero, having driven past the same fish and chip shop for the third time, summoned his courage to express a measure of doubt concerning their whereabouts.

'Oh, dear, dear, dear,' said George crossly. 'Haven't you been listening? . . . Stop the car – I'll pinpoint our position.'

With a window now open the smog disappeared sufficiently to reveal that they had come to a halt precisely opposite a sign which read:

'Aha,' exclaimed our navigator, snapping shut the map. 'Here we are then. No trouble at all. . . . Bring my bag will you, old man?' he called over his shoulder. 'Can't manage that damn boot of yours. You'll have to get it seen to, you know.'

Finally extricating his rear-seat passengers with no more than minor superficial damage to the roof light, Ralph was fortunate enough to find a parking space not more than a quarter of a mile away. However, with two bowls bags in addition to his own, and the blistering heat of the midday sun, he found the distance ample and sufficient.

Visiting teams are always assured of a warm welcome from the host club, and it was thus that our hero discovered his passengers – happily engaged in an exchange of friendly banter; idly sipping a refreshing cup of tea and nibbling a digestive biscuit.

Bowler-driver arriving at away fixture

'Oh, do come on, old man,' tutted George. 'Nearly time to start, you know. You're too late for tea.'

As Ralph cast a wistful eye at the empty biscuit plate, the tea lady was moved to squeeze just one last cup from the pot. It was barely lukewarm, but our perspiring hero gulped it gratefully, only to find that the kindly soul had been a trifle over-optimistic – barely submerged beneath the placid surface lurked a solid wodge of bloated tea leaves.

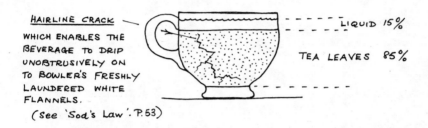

HAIRLINE CRACK
WHICH ENABLES THE
BEVERAGE TO DRIP
UNOBTRUSIVELY ON
TO BOWLER'S FRESHLY
LAUNDERED WHITE
FLANNELS.
(see 'Sod's Law'. P.53)

LIQUID 15%

TEA LEAVES 85%

Analysis of bowler-driver's welcoming beverage

As he followed his companions to the dressing room – chewing manfully on a mouthful of grouts – Ralph had to confess to certain reservations regarding the afternoon so far, and made one or two additional notes for future reference.

These notes will be of some service to the prospective bowler, who will have already perceived the wisdom of absolute secrecy regarding the possession of the motor car. Should this cunning deception be discovered, he is advised to trade it in at once for a dilapidated two-seater, complete with leaky hood – but *not* it is emphasized of the pick-up truck variety.

Determined and resourceful passengers, with waterproof apparel and umbrellas, may prove the leaky-roof theory to be counterproductive – in that the only occupant in grave danger of contracting pneumonia is the owner-driver. Consequently – on completing a full course of antibiotics and a brief convalescence – our new bowler may wish to proceed a step further towards the ultimate solution and adopt one or more of the following alternative solo transport modes.

Special note: Should none of the above prove acceptable, the bowler owner/driver should consider either:

(a)   Abject surrender – purchase second-hand chauffeur's cap
(b)   Take up Morris dancing

Ralph was fortunate to secure the last remaining peg in the dressing room. Perched precariously on one leg amid the spare mats and scoreboards, he was at least conveniently placed to overhear his friend George explaining to the Captain the reason for the lateness of Herbert's rink. Their driver, it appeared, was not only a timid and inept exponent, but totally devoid of any sense of direction.

By the time our hero, still perspiring a little, emerged from the clubhouse, the opposing captains had embarked upon their introductory speeches. These were blissfully brief; but before dismissing the players to their respective rinks, both concluded with the rider that they would have more to say at a later time. Subsequent events would reveal that this was no idle threat.

Bowlers rejoicing at the news that their captains will have more to say later

At the conclusion of a further bout of introductory handshaking, which had been such a feature of their arrival, Ralph was handed the jack. It is the custom for this courtesy to be accorded to the visitors, and our hero cast it with studied care to his favourite spot, only to see it kicked unceremoniously to full length.

His puckered brow was smoothed by the explanation that, in matches, players are permitted the luxury of two trial ends – one in each direction, for the purpose of:

(a) fetching short-sleeved pullover from dressing room
(b) spirited exchange of views on ineptitude of respective committees
  – with particular reference to not being selected as skip

(c)   relating somewhat risqué story regarding the commercial travel-
       ler and a lady acrobat from Singapore

(d)   adjusting dress for additional comfort, e.g. retying shoelaces;
       untwisting braces; hitching up underpants or rectifying inside-out
       sock

(e)   visiting lavatory

*Bowlers assessing correct line and pace of the green
during the trial ends*

Note: The trial end may also be used to assess the correct line and pace
of the green by concentrating on every wood bowled. However, in
Club Matches, this is liable to be regarded as an ostentatious display of
affectation, smacking of vulgar professionalism unworthy of the true
club bowler.

During the trial ends, and certainly before the game starts, it is
sound practice for the visiting side to initiate the opening gambit in the
spoken word by casting aspersions on the state of the host's green –
thus establishing an instant alibi in the event of losing. If, by any
chance, the visitors should emerge victorious, then the greater credit to
them.

The approach should on no account be openly rude or abrasive.
Such comments as:

(a)   'We could have played on my allotment.'

                          or

(b)   'Did they find what they were digging for?'

may prove counterproductive, in that they will provoke your hosts
into such prodigious feats that your club may well find itself on the
receiving end of a sound thrashing.

The best results are obtained from the sympathetic murmur, stemming from a genuine concern for the misfortune that has befallen your hosts. Recommended examples:

(a) 'What a shame. . . . You've taken expert advice, no doubt?'
(b) 'What a shame. . . . I can remember when we so looked forward to playing here.'
(c) 'What a shame. . . . Greenkeeper off sick, is he?' is a sure-fire winner.

The timing of this ploy is critical. Too soon, and it will lack credibility. Too late, and the home side will pre-empt the move by repeated declarations of how lucky they are to have such a green; coupled with the assertion that 'If you can't bowl on this, you can't bowl anywhere.' Such assertions are difficult to counter without resorting to vulgar squabbling, and our novice will observe the absolute necessity of 'getting in first'.

At the conclusion of the trial ends our heroes were to receive another surprise, when the No. 3s remained at the head with the skip. This is known as '3s up', the purpose of which is:

(a) to give the No. 3 a clearer picture of the head he is bowling to
(b) more importantly – in the best traditions of British sportsmanship – to reduce the unfair odds of 3 onto 1 against the skip to a sporting 2 against 2.
i.e., Front end (Nos. 1 and 2) *v.* Back end (No. 3 and Skip).

The game began. Herbert called for a short medium jack – thus ensuring that anything his team might have inadvertently learned from the trial ends was of no use whatsoever . . . and they were off.

Ralph, keyed up at the prospect of a higher standard of play, was not disappointed – certainly not at the quality of the spoken word. And in this respect, Herbert – still smouldering with resentment – stood head and shoulders above the rest with a virtuoso performance of excerpts from *The Skips' Manual of Scathing Comments*.

Beginners of a sensitive disposition should note that the main purpose behind such observations is to indicate to all within earshot – particularly members of the Selection Committee – that the skip is labouring under the handicap of a singularly inept team, and it will be by his efforts alone that disaster will be averted. Conversely, praise for good bowls will be considerably muted, lest the impression be given that he is having a soft time and there is nothing left for him to do.

But our aspiring bowlers should beware of generalizations. They will be called upon to serve before the mast under many types of skip, and it is essential that they are in a position to identify and counter the foibles and idiosyncrasies of this peculiar species – in whatever guise they may present themselves.

Skips – Classification Chart and Counter-measures

The Martinet

Hypercritical – sharp of tongue and abusive. Extensive repertoire of vitriolic comments. Praise for good bowl is absence of above. Fires a lot. Always last to finish due to inordinate number of 'no-ends'. Never has any matches.

Effect – terrifies most into bowling above themselves; reduces player of slightly nervous disposition to gibbering pulp.

Counter-measures – cringing servility. Seek to ingratiate yourself with sacrificial offerings of tobacco, alcohol and tempting sweetmeats. Eagerly proffer use of your lighter – for keeps.

or

Counter-attack with defiant insolence, thus establishing a bond of mutual admiration and respect, and making a friend for life.

Note: The female version or 'Martinette' (as illustrated) warrants a Government Health Warning.

Gentleman bowlers of a sensitive nature are advised to proceed with extreme caution.

The Christian

Very demonstrative. Claps a lot. Treats average bowls with effusive praise – bad bowls with a load of sanctimonious twaddle regarding their possible usefulness. Bowls his little heart out and readily accepts blame for humiliating defeats.

Effect – minimal, if not downright detrimental. His team wallow in smug complacency at not being able to bowl a bad wood, and get steadily worse as the game proceeds.

Counter-measures – none necessary. Do as you like.

The Martyr

Of glum disposition. Expects the worst – invariably gets it and rejoices. Unhappy if team bowling well. Peppermint sucker – acute dyspepsia. Never offers them round. *Effect* – good. Usually gets the best out of the team – especially the awkward customers who take great delight in bowling well and winning the game – thus denying their skip the joy of a mournful inquest on their ignominious defeat. *Counter-measures* – bowl well. Maintain a string of merry quips to ensure a jocular and happy atmosphere on your rink. Hide the peppermints.

The Weakling

Polite, considerate and indecisive. Asks his team's opinions and offers alternatives. As a concession he is allowed to chalk touchers. Recipient of vitriolic abuse if he doesn't draw the shot every end. *Effect* – chaotic. Internal dissension rife – open rebellion of front end. Power struggle develops; leadership usurped by dominant personality – often the No.2. *Counter-measure* – plunge into mêlée, or retire to the bank and do the crossword. If nursing secret ambitions to become a skip, scheme to be included in his rink every match. Golden opportunity for practice in the field.

The Corpse

Taciturn and immobile. Instructions limited to imperceptible movement of right index finger. All bowls – good and bad – acknowledged with barely discernible nod.

Effect – debilitating. Team never sure whether they are lying 3 up or 4 down. Opposition take possession of rink and spoken word.

Counter-measures – listen carefully to all comments from opposing skip to glean snippets of information regarding state of the head. Hold mirror in front of your leader's lips every two or three ends to check that respiration is still present.

The Ham

Excitable and neurotic. Oscillates rapidly between flights of extreme optimism and the depths of utter despair. Jumps about a lot.

Effect – unpredictable. Will win or lose by enormous margin. Team becomes jittery and hysterical – attempt wildly improbable and theatrical shots. On their lucky days will annihilate any opposition.

Counter-measures – enjoy the fun. Don't bother to draw, aim running bowls at the jack. Near misses provoke amazing acrobatic contortions well worth watching. Attempts at smashing all opponents' bowls out of the head also provide a most rewarding spectacle.

Ensure plentiful supply of throat lozenges – a continuous barrage of cheering and groaning adds a delightful touch to the proceedings.

But our thinking novice should beware of over-simplification. Skips – devious little devils that they are – can rarely be so neatly pigeon-holed. More often they are a subtle and unpredictable blend, and Herbert was no exception – alternating between the martinet and the martyr, with perhaps the merest *soupçon* of corpse.

Arnold, his opposite number, was a true Christian – that is in strictest bowling sense – but tinged with overtones of the weakling. This rare blend – a much sought after collector's item – is often strangely effective. The slap-happy effect of the former being countered by the sharpening of wits in the struggle to usurp his authority.

Our heroes were indeed fortunate to have this early opportunity of assessing the effectiveness of two such contrasting philosophies of leadership; and of observing at first hand the disparity between their individual selection of comments from the *Skips' Manual* with regard to bowls of identical quality.

Bowl	*Arnold* *(Christian/ Weakling)*	*Herbert* *(Martinet/Martyr)*
Two yards through	'Good back wood, Horace, never wasted there.'	'I'll do the firing.'
Yard wide	'Bad luck – perfect length; seems to hang out on that hand.'	'No, that was yesterday, we're on Rink 3 today.'
Two yards short	'Perfect line – I think the green is slowing up a bit.'	'Tell me about it – I can't see it from here.'
Too narrow	'Bad luck – I think you caught a run there.'	'That'll come in handy – they might trip over it.'
Too wide	'Good try – perfect weight. Little less green next time.'	'I should leave that there for when we go on tour.'
In the ditch	'Bad luck – lovely line. They just won't stop, will they?'	'That one for sale, is it?'

Wobbly delivery	'Bad luck, Horace. Woods are slippery today. Why don't you borrow my duster.'	'Did you take it out of its box?'
Draws shot	'That's the one. Great wood. Well bowled!'	'Thought you'd gone home.'
Draws another	'Brilliant! Well done. What a bowler.'	'Now you've given them a shoulder.'
Hits opponent in for shot	'Bad luck – couldn't be helped – only one down.'	'They've got a few vacancies. I'll get you a form.'
Hits own shot out	'Bad luck – worth a try – only three down.'	No comment – turns back and studies passing aeroplane.
Collides with previous short bowl	'What bad luck. You would have been right on the jack.'	'Got a little plan of our own, have we?'
Wrong bias	'Bad luck. My fault. I shouldn't have changed your hand.'	Renewed interest in plane – now from sitting position.

Martinet skip commenting on wrong bias

Our new bowler should not labour under the impression that the internal conflict is a one-sided affair, weighted entirely in favour of the skip and his accomplice. On the contrary, our heroes were much impressed by the ingenious ripostes of their more experienced front-end opponents in redressing the balance and establishing that:

(a) their feeble showing on this particular end had been an isolated lapse, and . . .
(b) that up to this point they themselves had been performing immaculately – but, sad to say, had not received the support they had the right to expect from their colleagues at the back end.

This direct frontal assault was further consolidated by an invidious sniping campaign of snide remarks, just audible enough to place their team-mates under even greater duress.

E.g. (i) 'Right. Well, let's see what they can do.'
(ii) 'Time they did something. Seven ends – they haven't drawn a shot yet.'
(iii) 'Keeping the best hand for themselves, are they?'
(iv) 'No match for their skip, is he?'
(v) 'If they can't draw that, they want to pack it in.'

Having listened dispassionately to both factions, Ralph felt unable to adjudicate between the contestants, and scored it as an honourable draw.

As the players acclimatized to the rink, the bowling improved; the heads became tighter and the roles of the No. 3s grew in importance. On their shoulders alone fell the responsibility of deciding amicably or otherwise – the result of each end.

The contest – although conducted in a dignified and civilized manner – invariably results in a steely clash of personalities as each strives to impose his will upon the other. Ralph observed closely, and was intrigued to witness the emergence of – if one may purloin a musical term – the dominant third.

It has been said that a good No. 3 is worth six shots a game to his side, but as the duel intensified it became increasingly apparent – to George's mounting exasperation – that their man was no match for the brusque, businesslike approach of his opponent.

'Three shots?' said the Parkview man, as the last wood came to rest. 'Agreed?' he added, swiftly kicking away the bowls in question, just as Stanley was opening his mouth to express some measure of doubt regarding the ownership of the second wood.

The rebuke he received from George was mild compared to Herbert's reaction. 'Three?' he snarled, fixing his No. 3 with a baleful glare. 'What are you playing at? . . . Do you give stamps as well?'

At the earliest opportunity, George – in a sneaky attempt to ingratiate himself with his skip – pointed out that the clown had lost them two shots on the previous end, and that his own speedy promotion to the position would prove of inestimable value to the club. But he had sadly miscalculated the situation; the back-end establishment closed ranks on him. 'Did he now?' growled Herbert. 'Well, perhaps if you were to get yours a bit closer we shouldn't need to measure, would we?'

And George retired with the proverbial flea in his ear.

No. 2 sneaking to his skip about their No. 3

Stanley, spurred on by his rebukes, stiffened his sinews and claimed four shots at the next end.

His opponent sucked his teeth. 'Mmmm. . . . Give you two,' he said, grudgingly kicking them out.

'And these,' chirruped our George, pouncing into the head and snatching up two more.

All eyes turned upon him in the silence.

'Ah,' said the Parkview man, brightening visibly. 'Ah. . . . Yes I thought you might want a measure on them. But now, of course. . . .' He shrugged and turned away, with a knowing wink at his team-mates.

Stanley glowered at our little fat friend. 'Two it is,' he sighed, and scurried off to sneak to Herbert about George.

No. 2 offering gratuitous but misguided assistance to his No. 3

And so, at this juncture, the score stood at 8–6 to Highcliffe, or as it might be more accurately expressed:

Stanley: 0 *v. Parkview No. 3*: 4

And, having observed how our tubby hero threw away the two shots that would have levelled the scores, our reader will readily draw the lesson: 'Look by all means – but do no touch.'

The following two ends were fairly uneventful, but the third was so close that our heroes were privileged to be present at the ceremony of measuring for the shot.

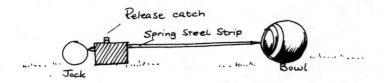

The measure

Our novice, if of an inventive turn of mind, might be interested to learn that a small fortune awaits the inventor of a measuring device that is at once foolproof – and cheat-proof.

It is not that any player wishes to hoodwink a fellow bowler – it is merely that he seeks to assess the mettle of his adversary, with regard to his eyesight, mental alertness and level of obstinacy. Downright cheating is not only unthinkable, but virtually impossible under the mistrustful and hawklike scrutiny of an experienced campaigner.

To the budding No. 3 our advice on the subject of measuring is much the same as *Punch*'s advice to those about to be married – '*Don't*'.

If you don't measure, you won't move the jack. And it is so easily done, with the tragic result that you will forfeit the shot you probably held, or concede to your opponents a shot that they probably didn't.

Measuring Guidelines
(for bowlers making their debut as No. 3)

(a) *When conceding shots*:   Insist upon the claimant measuring. 'If you want them, you measure them' is the maxim. Harden your heart to pleas of infirmity, senility, stupidity or 'Tippler's Twitch'.

(b) *When claiming shots*:   Attempt, by any devious means at your disposal, to persuade your opponent to manipulate the measure. (Arthritic knee is a useful ploy – not forgetting to limp for the next few days.)

(c) Never, under any circumstances, accept the offer of your opponent's measure – it will invariably possess mechanical defects which will ensure you move the jack.

(d) Make certain that your own measure possesses a range of peculiar quirks and idiosyncrasies which render it tricky to use. Press it upon your opponent on every conceivable occasion.

(e) While opponent is measuring, maintain a constant banter of helpful advice and constructive criticism with regard to his technique. When his hands begin to tremble with irritation movement of the jack is imminent. Press home the advantage.

Special note:

(i) *If you think opponents just hold* – Do not despair. Press for an endless succession of remeasuring by all and sundry in the faint hope that the jack will eventually be moved towards your bowl. If it isn't, nothing is lost.

(ii) *If you think that you just hold* – Oppose fiercely any attempt at remeasuring. Summon neutral umpire at once. Preferably one closely related, or at least known to be favourably disposed to your side.

Determined as they may be, it is inevitable that our embryo No. 3s will encounter equally astute opponents and, unless the game is to grind to a halt in a state of deadlock, they will be forced to employ their measures. Against this eventuality, they are advised to study the following section.

The Art of Measuring: Elementary Standard or Underhand Method

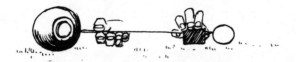

Scrupulously fair. Opponent is afforded clear view of both extremities of measure. Tape is straight and true, and offered to nearest points of both jack and bowl.

A method employed by all high-principled and clean-living No. 3s – and in all contests between evenly matched opponents who have tested each other out, and concluded that neither is going to fall for any little bits of 'monkey business' on the part of the other.

Variations on Standard Method – in order of ascending subtlety; invaluable for assessing the quality of the opposition.

(a) *Basic Radial Ploy*

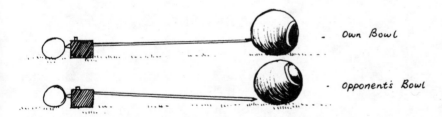

- *Own Bowl*

- *Opponents Bowl*

Very amateurish, but worth a try as an opening gambit. If you can get away with this, you can get away with anything.

(b) *Overhand Ploy*

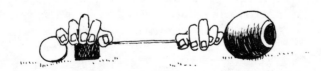

Ensures that at no stage of the proceedings is your opponent able to catch the merest glimpse of *either* end of the measure.

The Art of Measuring: Advanced Level for Mature Students Only

(c) *Kinky Ploy*

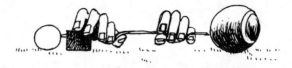

Skilful exponent can achieve deviation of + or − 1in per foot – but not recommended for beginners. Demands high degree of manual dexterity – piano lessons an advantage.

Ralph, hitherto absorbed by this power struggle, suddenly realized that, for some time now, George had been maintaining a low profile. Doubtful that his friend's strange behaviour was attributable to his earlier rebuke, our kindly hero concluded that he must be feeling unwell. He had need of no such worries.

George, ever alert to the main chance, had become preoccupied and intrigued by the possibilities of what we shall refer to as the:

Running After Bowl Syndrome

Our astute entrepreneur had observed that deliveries enthusiastically pursued by the bowler appeared, by and large, to turn out far better than those which proceeded on their appointed course without the assistance of pounding feet close behind – an unfortunate misinterpretation, sadly only too common among raw beginners.

Should any of our own readers harbour aspirations to become a 'runner' they must guard against labouring under our hero's misapprehension, and acquaint themselves with the governing principles of 'running after bowl'.

(a) Delay start of your sprint until you are sure the bowl is a good one. Experience and practice will reduce your assessment time.

(b) Never run after a bad bowl. Arriving simultaneously at the head with a pitiful effort can prove highly embarrassing and expose you to ridicule.

Medical note: Before attempting this manoeuvre our novice is advised to present himself for a thorough medical examination to verify his physical condition. Collapsing en route in a breathless heap, and completing the trip, gasping and wheezing on all fours, will detract from the desired overall impression.

Having grasped the elementary principles, the keen student will soon master the art of selecting which bowls to pursue and which to ignore. Even so, the occasional misjudgement is inevitable. But all is not lost. Such errors, as always, can be salvaged by the judicious application of the spoken word which should at all times accompany the pursued bowl.

Spoken Word (Running After Bowl)

(a) Good bowl   Comment unnecessary – confine to gentle murmurs of encouragement. Lengthen stride and accelerate to arrive simultaneously with bowl, to receive, with due modesty, the plaudits of your team-mates.

(b) Short bowl   Quick thinking required. Decelerate rapidly and switch to 'intended blocker' ploy. Cries of 'Stay', 'Stop there' and 'That should do it' should establish beyond reasonable doubt that your aim has been accomplished.

(c) Too wide   Screech to a halt on the instant of realization and switch to 'tactical' ploy: 'Off that one', 'Half ball' or 'Don't make a shoulder' can be gainfully employed. Retreat hurriedly to the mat, turning a deaf ear to derisory catcalls and jeers from your colleagues.

(d) Too heavy   Cries of 'That's it – right through' and 'Go on – round the back' may convince sceptical colleagues that a back bowl was your intention, certainly nothing as boringly mundane as drawing the shot. Run past them with your bowl – avoid eye contact.

(e) Bad bowl	If too bad for any application of the 'spoken word', bluff it out. Shout derogatory cry of 'Rubbish!' before anyone else does, stifling further abuse with the rider: 'Everyone's entitled to one a game.' Thereby establishing that, up to this point, you have been playing an absolute blinder.

New bowlers, in the sunset years of their retirement, and long past the peak of condition, need not despair.

Although lacking the fleetness of foot and stamina for the full distance, they can still make a worthwhile contribution to their side by mastering the technique of the 'part runner' or 'lolloper'.

Part Running (Lolloping)

After delivering his bowl, the skilful exponent will set off at a lolloping trot, stuttering to a halt – in a flagrant defiance of the Laws of the Game – at a point approximately halfway up the green. This not only obscures the track and destination of his bowl from his opponent, but keeps him fretting impatiently on the mat while the lolloper ambles back to his place.

Constant repetition of this ploy will provoke his opposite number into a state of seething irritability, and the subsequent deterioration of his play could be worth several shots to our lolloper's rink.

With assiduous practice he can introduce a further refinement to his technique by veering off at a tangent to come to a halt on – or if possible – just over the boundary string.

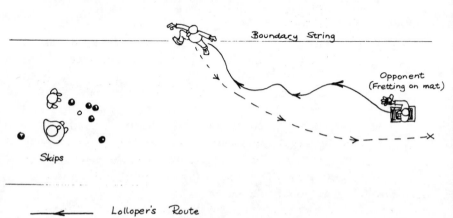

Boundary String

Opponent
(Fretting on mat)

Skips

Lolloper's Route

Return Route (obscuring opponent's view of the head.)

This enables him not only to obtain a clearer picture of the head, but to cause considerable frustration and inconvenience to players on the next rink.

If our lolloper is sufficiently versatile to utilize both forehand and backhand, he should succeed in infuriating opponents on both adjoining rinks, thus enhancing the prospect of an overall victory for his club.

Having given due consideration to this 'running' business, George decided it was high time that he, too, made his mark; to establish himself as a cut above his somewhat pedestrian front-end colleagues, content to remain upon the mat and accept that humble station in life to which they had been called.

His take-off and initial acceleration was not particularly noteworthy, but once his ample girth had attained full momentum his little legs twinkled along at a spanking pace.

Unfortunately, it had been some time since he had taken to his heels, in deadly earnest and the mathematical equation relating to 'mass times velocity' had slipped his mind. In consequence, he had gravely underestimated his optimum braking distance.

This miscalculation was confirmed by the look of blind panic on his face as – eyes boggling and clutching desperately at the air – he sped past the head; cleared the ditch with a despairing bound and disappeared through the clubhouse door.

His sudden entrance – unexpected and unannounced – precipitated some measure of astonishment among the tea ladies, going quietly about their business. And it was indeed fortunate that the Captain's lady wife had the presence of mind to fling open the kitchen door to allow him free passage, thus saving the home club considerable expenditure on the replacement of various items of their best match crockery.

Our novice, if wishing to be a 'runner' and still retain the goodwill of his fellows, should be at pains to observe the etiquette – not to mention the Laws – by ensuring that when his bowl comes to rest he is either behind the mat or behind the head. But there is no need to carry the matter to extremes.

As Herbert cuttingly observed when our hero, somewhat sheep-faced and breathless, eventually rejoined his unit: 'Well, you got behind the head, lad. . . . No need to get behind the car park.'

Ralph, having witnessed his colleague's ill-fated expedition, resolved to defer any similar extravagances until he had gained more experience. And the wisdom of this decision was confirmed almost immediately by an incident which may serve as a cautionary tale to the thoughtful student.

Having listened patiently to his skip's desperate use of the 'spoken word' as he pursued a succession of particularly poor efforts, Ralph's opposing No. 1 could contain himself no longer. 'Do you know something, Percy?' he observed sagely. 'It's a strange thing . . . every time you bowl a bad 'un – the ruddy thing goes deaf.'

The rest of the game passed without major incident. Our heroes' rink, with George claiming the lion's share of the credit, slipped steadily behind and finished a dozen or so shots down. Proceedings were brought to a close by yet another outburst of hand pumping, at the conclusion of which they were introduced to yet another feature of the club match, i.e., bowling the woods back for 'a penny on the jack – nearest takes all'.

The full credit for this amusing and highly diverting little ritual must be given to the originators of the game who – mischievous little devils – decided that the game should be played over an odd number of ends, thus ensuring that the players should endure the maximum inconvenience by finishing at the furthermost point from both the clubhouse and their assorted paraphernalia and hand luggage.

Ralph, conscientious soul that he was, applied himself diligently to the task, and was somewhat mystified at the lackadaisical approach of the old hands whom he suspected of not trying too hard.

Naturally he won. But as he peered through the now thickening drizzle to receive his plaudits, he was further puzzled to observe his fellow players scurrying for the shelter of the dressing room with parting exhortations to: 'Bring the mats, will you?' and 'Don't forget the scoreboard, old man.'

His shirt clung to his shoulders and the first rivulet trickled down his neck. And as he grovelled around the rink to locate the carelessly flung coins, a glimmer of suspicion clouded his brow.

Winner of 'penny on the jack' savouring his moment of triumph

He hurried after them as best he could, laden as he was with bowls, jack, mats and a cast-iron scoreboard of early Victorian design, only for his earlier suspicions to be confirmed by the news that it was traditional for all such monies to be contributed to the charity box.

He complied with his customary good grace, even forcing a wan smile, but even as he did so he made yet another mental note to add to his jottings.

Our astute reader will resolve on all 'POJ' occasions, to position his woods at some considerable distance from the jack. But on no account bowl short – some practical joker is sure to knock it in for shot. As a general principle observe the maxim: 'In the ditch is the only real safeguard.'

Aprés Bowl
(with apologies to Winter Sports enthusiasts)

The aprés match procedure may be grouped under three main headings:

(a) The Meal
(b) The Spoken Word (Speeches)
(c) Chat and Departure

and it is incumbent upon our novice to acquaint himself with the protocol which accompanies this procedure in order that he may be spared the embarrassment of committing any social indiscretion, in breach of the established etiquette.

Section I: The Meal

Having accepted a drink from his opposite number, our novice should on no account attempt to dally at the bar for a few snifters and a social chat, but should hasten to his place at the table where he will discover his colleagues already seated; fidgeting restlessly with cutlery poised anxious to begin the main business of the day.

He must understand that the basis of the Club Match is 'going out to tea', delayed by the tiresome intrusion of a couple of hours' bowling, before the gastric juices can be allowed full rein.

Confirmation of this proposition may be obtained by:

(a) observing the abundance of names on the availability list for matches against clubs renowned for the quality of their teas

(b) enquiries regarding how the club fared in last week's match. Such replies as:

'Not bad – the lettuce was a bit soggy.'

or

'Nice piece of ham, but too many pips in the jam.'

will give our beginner some indication of the order of priorities.

Cautionary note:

Our reader will observe the reference to lettuce and ham, and at this point it is only fair to advise our aspiring bowler that he should, without delay, take steps to cultivate an insatiable appetite for the salad meal.

Should he be allergic – nay, indifferent even – to such fare, he is advised to give serious consideration to his suitability for the game, and to contemplate seeking his relaxation in a less exacting pastime.

The bowler is called upon to consume copious quantities of salad throughout the season. Indeed, it has been estimated that, in the course of his career, the indefatigable match player will consume upwards of half an acre of lettuce, and our novice is urged to be ever watchful for any changes in his facial appearance.

There are those among us whose metabolism is unable to cope with such a high lettuce intake, and it would be sad if our novice – having eluded the dreaded 'Bowler's Hand' and 'Novice's Foot' – should be struck down with the fearsome salad malady, commonly known as 'Bowler's Bunny'.

Beginner   After 5 years   After 10 years.

Indefatigable match bowler

Constant vigilance is necessary to spot the onset of the affliction; the earliest symptom being a tendency to twitch the nose to relieve a slight itchiness. To arrest and reverse the process, the bowler should cut down his availability for matches to every other game. If the condition has been neglected, to one in three.

Only a digestive system in tip-top condition affords an effective resistance to the sickness, and – with the wellbeing of our reader in mind – his attention is drawn to the following.

Cautionary notes:

(a) Each season, in addition to the lettuce, the devoted match player will be called upon to devour some $3\frac{1}{2}$ yards of cucumber, and our raw recruit – even under the most searching interrogation – is warned against confessing to the slightest partiality for the stuff.

Should you display the slightest hesitancy, you will find your plate heaped high with the allotted portions of your table mates, anxious to avoid further damage to their digestive tracts, and ruthless in their determination to eliminate the risk of terminal cucumber.

Plate of unsuspecting novice after foolishly confessing to fondness for the occasional slice of cucumber

(b) Do not, certainly for the first few matches, attempt to emulate the gastronomic feats of your more experienced colleagues, particularly those who have spent most of the afternoon bewailing their recent loss of appetite, delicate constitution and general debility.

The brisk despatch of a hearty salad, spring and pickled onions, strawberry jam, home-made scones and fruit cake, washed down with alternate swigs of good strong ale and a mug of hot sweet tea, rounded off with a nice piece of cheese and a handful of biscuits, is not a matter to be taken lightly by our raw recruit.

A gradual build-up is recommended, bringing your digestive organs to peak fitness before attempting to compete on level terms with your ailing companions.

Special note: Match Tea Ham, being the price it is, is carved only by master craftsmen working to the finest of tolerances and observing the criterion that '. . . it shall be of a thickness which allows the small ads in the *Daily Telegraph* to be easily read through a single slice laid upon the page.'

Our novice, if particularly partial to a nice piece of ham, is urged to rest his cutlery upon it at the earliest opportunity, lest the draught from a nearby window should waft the succulent morsel onto an adjoining plate. From whence – without a degree of unpleasantness – it may prove difficult for the rightful owner to effect recovery.

Bowlers disputing rightful ownership of tasty morsel of ham

Our hero, deprived of the benefit of these cautionary notes, had slipped up rather badly on all three counts and was, as a result, feeling a little queasy. But the contemplation of his indiscretions was rudely interrupted by the loud rapping of a knife handle on the table top.

The measured solemnity of the knocking – somewhat reminiscent of Black Rod's arrival at the Upper Chamber for the State Opening of Parliament – indicated that the fulfilment of the captain's earlier threats was now imminent.

Section II: The Speeches

The spoken word, hitherto merely an optional extra, now assumes its rightful pride of place, and our novice should come to terms with the established dictum:

'When two or three bowlers are gathered together in my sight, one of them will make a speech.' (Quite possibly, all of them.)

Our heroes were to receive verification of this fact as the Home Captain, for the thirty-seventh time that season, rose wearily to his feet to deliver the obligatory 'few words'.

Ralph, dear reactionary old soul, was much moved by the dignity of the ceremony, marred just a trifle perhaps by the fact that the Host Captain had not only forgotten the name of his opposite number but, having mistaken the date, was under the misapprehension that they had been playing against a different club altogether.

Captain: 'Captain er . . . er . . . (*scratches head thoughtfully – gives up*) . . . and er . . . members of the Snodbury Bowling Club.' (*His Hon.Sec. and right-hand man groaned softly and tugged gently at his leader's sleeve . . .*)

Hon.Sec.: (*whispering*) 'Highcliffe.'
(*Unfortunately, having thoughtlessly taken his seat adjacent to his captain's deaf ear, the process of correcting this minor hiccup served only to aggravate the situation.*)

Captain: (*ploughing on*) 'It is with great pleasure . . .'

Hon.Sec.: (*louder*) 'Highcliffe.'

Captain: '. . . that we welcome our old friends from . . .'

Hon.Sec.: (*elbowing captain viciously in ribs*) 'Highcliffe!'
(*A moment's silence – Captain peers blankly at Hon.Sec.*)

Captain: 'Eh?'

Hon.Sec.: (*enunciating very slowly and clearly*) 'Highcliffe. They're from Highcliffe.'

Captain: 'Who?'

Hon.Sec.: (*bellowing*) 'Highcliffe!!!'

Captain: (*pausing to adjust deaf aid*) 'Cliff?'
(*The Hon.Sec. sighed with relief and nodded eagerly*)

Captain: 'Ah yes. Of course . . . sorry. Silly of me . . . er . . . Captain Cliff. . . .'

Hon.Sec.: 'Oh, God.' (*buries head in hands*)

Lest our novice be tempted to adopt a scornful attitude, he would be well advised to recall the words of the immortal Gilbertian lyric – slightly amended herein, with abject apologies to devotees of the Savoy Operettas – contending that: 'A captain's lot is not a happy one . . . happy one . . .' and to remember that the luckless fellow has been raised to his exalted position more as a result of his good-natured gullibility than his powers of oratory.

Sympathy and tolerance should be the watchwords – carefully noting that the slightest hint of criticism on the part of our novice will find him landed with the job much sooner than he bargains for.

Recovering well from his somewhat shaky start, the Home Captain pulled himself together and gave a workmanlike, if unspectacular, rendering of the *Aprés Match Stock Speech*.

It is not our intention to dwell at length upon the contents of this little gem. Two or three matches should be sufficient for the average beginner to familiarize himself with the salient points, together with the minor variations encompassing:

(a)   Home/Away
(b)   Winning/Losing
(c)   Start/Middle/End of season

It is apposite at this juncture to point out that bowlers taking a full and active part in matches and the social activities of their clubs will be required, in any one season, to absorb something in the region of 120 speeches, or to express it more accurately, the same speech 120 times.

Cautionary note:
Potential bowlers, uncertain whether they possess sufficient strength of character to withstand such an onslaught on both eardrum and nervous system, should once again question their true fitness for the game. Many a promising beginner, lacking the necessary moral fibre, has fled the clubhouse, never to return, after a mere twenty or thirty repetitions.

Listening: The Role of the Recipient

New bowlers, fresh from the more boisterous games of their youth in which the spoken word played a distinctly lesser role, may need to modify their general conduct. Yawning, stretching and fidgeting on the uncompromising club chairs are not welcome. Etiquette – whilst not demanding that anyone actually listens – does require a certain stillness.

CORRECT   INCORRECT

Likewise, derisory jeers, catcalling and the projection of any form of missile are most definitely out of order.

Verification of this edict came to Ralph as, glancing furtively around, he noticed among the throng a sprinkling of old contemporaries from his far-off footballing days – greying and balding now, and decidedly more rotund, but instantly recognizable.

As he studied their passive demeanour he could not but reflect on the mellowing effect of the passing years, and the steadying influence of a game for true gentlemen.

His memory stirred to recall the last occasion on which he had been afforded the dubious honour of addressing a few words to such a gathering, at the Annual Football Club Supper, and had foolishly exceeded his allotted two minutes.

Were these the same fellows? he mused. The same high-spirited lads who, having failed to silence him with hoots of derision and a hail of boiled potatoes and soggy rolls, had brought his little homily to a swift and sudden end by divesting him of his trousers and anointing his bare backside with a pint of best bitter before hurling him through the clubhouse door.

Ah . . . time passes, he reflected, gazing again upon the placid faces. But his nostalgic reverie was shattered by another burst of enthusiastic applause.

The beginner should observe that he will be required to clap a lot. Thwarted by the sheer practical difficulties of shaking the speaker warmly by the hand, the bowler settles for the comforting substitute of banging them together.

In this matter great care should be exercised by our pupil, and he is advised to take his lead from his more experienced companions. A generous round of applause may persuade the reluctant orator that he has said enough, and eagerly resume his seat. If carried to excess, however, he may be tempted to entertain delusions of grandeur which could result in a lengthy ordeal for all concerned.

The whole subject of appreciative applause leads us, in the natural order of things, to digress for a moment. It is inevitable that among our readers will be a small core of ambitious beginners, eager and determined to get to the top of the bowling tree, and it is in their interests that the following section is included.

Special note: It is *not* for the majority of our readers – the 'wasters' and 'ne'er do wells' – whose aims are merely to enjoy the game; make a host of good friends; perhaps win a bob or two occasionally and, if blessed with the necessary talent, get to the top by virtue of their own bowling ability. Such people neither deserve nor, in fact, do they need any advice from the likes of us.

Career Bowler: Aprés Match Technique

Having infiltrated the big match (by various means to be outlined in a later work) our career novice will observe that the modest spectacle of a couple of bumbling captains has been replaced by an impressive top table arrayed with VIPs, all of whom may be pressed into saying a few impromptu words, based on the copious notes piled before them.

It is upon this scene that our ambitious bowler can truly make his mark. An indifferent performance on the green, where he has failed to draw a shot all the afternoon, can frequently be rectified by an inspired performance at the tea table.

But frantic and impassioned applause – praiseworthy though it may be – is not enough. And to bring a sense of discipline and purpose to his efforts, our ambitious novice is advised to study the following guidelines:

(a) *Positional play* Be first to the table, select seat with care. The finest virtuoso performance will be valueless if concealed from the top table by fat bowler with protruding ears.

Note: If thwarted in the attempt to secure a recommended seat (having been outwitted by more experienced opponents) *do not* dissipate your energies on a lost cause, but await a more propitious occasion.

But having secured, by fair means or foul, a commanding field of fire, our ambitious student is now in a position to press home his advantage!

(b) *Posture* – Do not lounge. Lean the trunk forward. Head slightly inclined; mouth slightly open, thereby displaying your intention of hanging upon every word with eager anticipation.

(c) *Timing* – Do not waste your time applauding with everyone else.

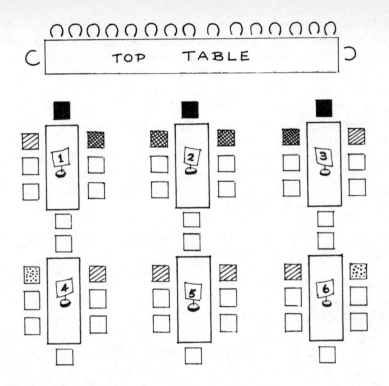

RECOMMENDED SEATS — KEY TO STARTING GRID

■   *Excellent. Prime seats. Pole positions*

▨   *Very good*

▧   *Fair — extra effort required*

▒   *Possible — worth a try — but unpromising*

☐   *Useless*

Big match — typical seating lay-out

   (i) Be first off the mark — concentrate on minor points which few will consider worthy of note.

  (ii) During general applause — freewheel. Conserve energy until applause wanes then redouble efforts. Continue after everyone else has stopped and speaker's eye is caught.

(d) *Style* — Practice to perfect an individual and instantly identifiable style. A slow rhythmic beat is both economical and dignified — cupping the hands gives greater resonance and a majestic timbre.

(e) *Vocal embellishments*   – Whistling, foot stamping and throwing cap in the air are not in order, but a generous sprinkling of 'Hear! Hear!'s and the occasional 'Bravo!' does not come amiss. As in (c) (i), employ only in quieter moments unworthy of general acclamation.

(f) *Humour*   – On this point our novice is urged to proceed with extreme caution. The jocular aprés match sally, often inaudible and frequently unintelligible, is difficult to identify. Whilst there is undoubted value in being the first one (possibly the only one) to spot the merry jest, it must be weighed against the pitfall of possible error.

A misplaced guffaw at a moment of sincere tenderness and maudlin sentimentality can precipitate a withering glare, and prove a crippling blow to our student's career prospects.

If in doubt, play safe. Delay reaction until general sycophantic merriment confirms existence of joke, but do not, under any circumstances, join in late. This may provoke misgivings on the question of your mental agility, and brand you a 'thicky'.

For such occasions, the true career bowler is never without an oversized and brightly patterned spare handkerchief with which, whilst doubled up with silent mirth, he can make great play of wiping away the tears of silent laughter. As the general merriment subsides, a final trumpeting blow of the nose adds a nice touch to round off the performance in impeccable style – as the envious scowls of his outmanoeuvred rivals will confirm.

Ambitious bowler responding to mildly amusing remark by County Acting Junior Deputy Assistant Hon.Treasurer

The exhausting demands of the big match tea will tax the career bowler's resources to breaking point, and unless he is mindful of both his mental and physical fitness he is liable to flag long before the finishing post hoves in sight.

Mental Agility and Concentration

In order to nurse his stamina, our student must be at pains to identify and classify each speaker, and thus avoid dissipating his energies on those whose influence on his future career will be minimal.

Total concentration and a measure of circumspection is the order of the day. For as the speakers rise and subside with the regularity of figures on a mechanical steam organ, the possibilities of human error increase to the point where even the most experienced exponents – wilting under the strain – have been prone to mis-read the situation.

Indeed on one occasion, in the midst of some confusion as to whose turn it was next, the visitors' coach driver – tentatively approaching the top table to confirm the exact time of departure – was surprised, but highly gratified, to receive an invitation to address a few words to the assembled gathering.

This he did with remarkable aplomb. And his impromptu discourse on the advantages of the modern diesel engine was accorded a standing ovation from a misguided group of career bowlers, under the impression that he was, in fact, a recently appointed member of the County Selection Committee.

Physical Fitness

The dedicated career bowler will be ever mindful of the need to maintain the hands in the peak of condition. Only by constant and assiduous clapping practice can a resonant, rhythmic timbre be perfected, and the soft flesh hardened and calloused to withstand the rigours of the occasion.

But individual practice is best undertaken in seclusion. If performed in conjunction with normal practice on the green, it is liable to attract unwelcome attention, and a measure of ridicule from the 'wasters' and 'ne'er do wells' lacking true appreciation of the finer points of the game.

For readers with a political bent, attendance at the Annual Conference of any of the major political parties is highly recommended. The prolonged ovations offer an invaluable opportunity for intensive stamina practice.

Extra Special Note (Financial)

The ailing career bowler, lacking the necessary physique and stamina, but blessed with adequate means, will derive some consolation from the fact that the despatch of a steady stream of gins and tonic in the direction of the top table will prove equally efficacious in the furtherance of his career prospects.

But we have digressed enough . . . and we rejoin the mainstream of the bowling world at the point when the captains' speeches had limped haltingly to their eventual conclusion, and the Highcliffe man had thankfully resumed his seat. Not to the usual tumultuous reception . . . but in total and terrifying silence!

Ralph, hands poised and ready to give vent to a burst of loyal approbation, was silenced by the admonishing glares of friend and foe alike. He looked anxiously around. . . . Something was amiss.

From all quarters came deep rumblings of discontent. Throats were cleared with coughs heavy with rebuke, and pointing fingers sawed the air with frantic signals.

Let us hasten to explain to our baffled reader that, in matters of his speech, the Captain will be forgiven for any slip of the tongue, social gaffe or cutting insult, inadvertent or otherwise. All will be overlooked, except the one cardinal sin of the visiting captain – he had forgotten to thank the ladies for the tea!

Luckless captain forgetting to thank the ladies for the tea

But a moment elapsed before the realization of his heinous offence came upon him. Leaping to his feet – red-faced and perspiring with embarrassment – he flung himself upon their mercy.

Hell hath no fury like a tea lady scorned but, with a depth of low cunning which belied his cherubic countenance, he won back the hearts of the grim-faced wives by artfully referring to them as the members' daughters, and displaying a measure of shocked disbelief at their coy and simpering denials.

Grovelling in a frenzy of self-abasement, he heaped effusive praise upon every single ingredient, including the pepper and salt, and sat down to a reception that rattled the very windows.

Honour was satisfied. Diplomatic relations were restored. The members were released from the bonds of formality, and set free to embark upon the final phase of the Aprés Match Procedure.

Chat and Departure

It is at this point that the true fellowship and bonhomie of the game reaches its peak. The rinks huddle together, glasses are charged and the air is filled with the hubbub of animated chatter as each in turn regales the company with tales of monstrous strokes of ill fortune which have bedevilled him over the years – without which a succession of major triumphs in the County Championships would have been his for the taking.

Tankards, tobacco tins and sundry impedimenta are requisitioned to indicate the precise position of the bowls at the critical moment when this skip sent up this dreadful wood – 'wicked' off this short bowl and. . . .

Postmortem: Bowler demonstrating diabolical 'wick' off short bowl

As Ralph listened attentively, he was swayed to the view that a game of bowls is rarely won by the better team, and that the outcome of all major competitions is decided by that unpredictable little quirk referred to, with much grinding of teeth, as the 'wick'.

George, who had mastered this particular shot on his very first day, saw nothing remarkable in this observation, and promptly rearranged the tankards to demonstrate how he had actually drawn a shot, a week ago last Tuesday.

When pressed on the matter, it emerged that the jack had, in fact, been flicked some four feet sideways to our stout friend's stray wood. Nevertheless, he had played a drawing bowl. It had ended up shot. Therefore, ipso facto, he had drawn the shot. On this point, George was adamant.

As the nectar of grape and grain flows ever more freely, fact merges with fiction, and absolute truth becomes a shade more elusive. Distance, coupled with a measure of exaggeration, lends enchantment, and embellishes those time-honoured stories from the past. Through a rosy haze of times remembered, life-long friendships are cemented, new friendships are born, and the din is indescribable.

But, alas, not all can participate to the full. Let us pause a moment to consider the plight of those subdued figures scattered here and there in the midst of the hurly-burly. Let our hearts go out to this little band – the conscientious law-abiding bowler-drivers – gazing wistfully upon the foaming tankards whilst sipping their lukewarm orange squash.

Aptitude Test No. 2: Can you spot the bowler-driver?

Ralph strove manfully to maintain a brave and cheerful face but when, at long last, his elderly opponent rose somewhat unsteadily to his feet and announced his departure – in order to take his good lady to the Old Tyme Dance – our hero was not too displeased. He felt that he had fully observed his social obligations, and wishing to indicate that he, too, was ready to make a move he rose from his chair.

His own unsteadiness was in no way attributable to inebriation, but to the problem of maintaining one's equilibrium with something approaching half a gallon of orange squash sloshing and slurping about in one's innards.

But one glance at his passengers was sufficient to persuade our hero that his vision of imminent departure might need to be modified. With brimming tankards, and the next round already lined up, it was obvious that they had not, as yet, given the matter any serious consideration.

Bowler-driver suggesting the possibility of going home

'Going?' said George, blinking owlishly in sheer disbelief.

'Going?' said Herbert gruffly, nearly spilling his ale.

'Going?' said Stanley.

The very idea was dismissed out of hand.

'Nonsense,' said George. 'Good Lord, man. No hurry is there? Sit down a minute, old chap. Have another squash.'

Ralph shuddered at the prospect, excused himself politely, and retired to a quiet corner for a few moments of tranquil contemplation and a chance to allow his stomach to come to rest.

A hand clamped itself on his shoulder. 'It's not . . . is it?'

Ralph looked up. 'Good Lord – Smithy! Do you know I thought it was you but I couldn't be sure. . . .'

'Manning – Ralph Manning!' exclaimed Smithy, snapping his fingers in triumph. 'Christ, you look old.'

'I've got more bloody hair than you,' retorted our hero, prodding his old comrade firmly in the chest.

'See who's over there?' Smithy pointed out a rather portly and distinguished-looking gentleman, propped against the bar in regal splendour, holding court for a little band of devotees who hung upon his every word.

Ralph frowned in semi-recognition.

'You remember,' prompted Smithy. 'Peter – Peter York.'

'Never,' said Ralph. 'That's never old Spotty! Good God, look at the size of him.'

'Hey, Yorky. Come here,' called Smithy. 'Look what I've found.'

Spotty's face lit up. He dismissed his disciples with a peremptory gesture and, within moments, one of the finest half-back lines ever to grace the Third Division of the Snodbury and District Sunday League was reunited for the first time in nearly thirty years.

Instantly time rolled back. The present evaporated in the warm glow of reminiscence. And with it, sad to say, evaporated our hero's praiseworthy alcoholic resolutions.

His old team-mates recoiled in revulsion at the sight of the orange squash and, despite Ralph's feeble and unconvincing protestations, it was replaced by a beverage more appropriate to the occasion.

It must be confessed that it was followed by several more, lubricating the memory to recall the halcyon days of yore.... 'Do you remember when? ... And that night we put that bloater in Muffin's bed.... And what about old Scotty and that Swedish bird when he.... And the night we won the cup and the vicar came in and ... whatever happened to old Muffin ...?'

Ralph was in his element. He felt twenty years younger, and was well set for the evening when a harsh jarring note impinged upon the proceedings.

'I think we'll make a move now, laddie.'

There was no mistaking George's authoritative tone. Ralph winced, and looked around to behold the spectacle of his entire retinue of passengers, booted and spurred, and ready for departure.

At Yorky's instigation, an attempt was made to ignore the situation. But it was no use. The glum trio, looming over them like harbingers of doom, cast a blight over our merry little band. Ralph, increasingly aware of three pairs of eyes boring into the back of his neck, gulped down his pint and, with mutual affirmations to keep in touch, went off to fetch his bag.

*

Passengers: indicating to bowler-driver that the moment for departure had now arrived

'Still raining,' said George, as our hero discovered them waiting in the porch. 'Pop and get the car, old man. No point in all of us getting wet.'

The journey home proved even more circuitous than the outward trip, involving a succession of detours to visit most of the Public Conveniences in the area, on account of the weakness of Herbert's bladder.

However, this did allow ample time for George to preside over an exhaustive postmortem on the afternoon's game, in the course of which he felt compelled to observe that if the other three had played as well as him the end result would have been far different. In this view he was unshakeable.

Nevertheless, he was of the opinion that all was not lost. As they got on so well together, he felt that they should keep the rink together and build for the future. Ralph groaned inwardly at the prospect.

Warming to his task, George proceeded to expound upon the course of action he thought they should follow, indicating that serious consideration might be given to rearranging the playing order – and admitting that, if pressed, he would be prepared to assume the mantle of skip.

In view of the difficult driving conditions of darkness and driving rain, our little fat friend – in addition to acting as discussion leader – felt obliged to extend his role of navigator to embrace the duties of co-driver, and rendered invaluable assistance by constantly fiddling with the heater controls, so that they oscillated rapidly between perspiring freely in sub-tropical conditions, and freezing in a succession of icy blasts.

These temperature fluctuations, coupled with the efforts of Herbert and his pipe, soon fogged the windscreen with a thick layer of condensation, and our intrepid travellers suffered a succession of very near squeaks as the co-driver – ever resourceful and alert to the danger – insisted on obliterating the driver's field of vision with vigorous manipulations of a large cloth.

Co-driver assisting bowler-driver in inclement weather conditions

'Look out!' cried Ralph, swerving violently to avoid separating the local constable from his bicycle. 'I can't see a thing,' he wailed.

'Can't see?' said George. 'Oh, dear. . . . Eyes giving you trouble, old man?' he enquired suspiciously, and promptly redirected his attention to violent manipulations of the headlamp switches in order – by a process of trial and error – to get a little more light on the subject.

But all good things come to an end and, having finally deposited his companions at all points of the compass, our hero, with a sigh of relief, drew to a halt at his front gate. Pausing awhile to regain his composure, and glancing around to assess the full extent of the internal damage, his gaze fell upon the petrol gauge.

He tapped it gently with his knuckle. And then again, harder. He had thoroughly enjoyed his first club match, but the consumption of approximately $2\frac{1}{2}$ gallons, for a trip to a club not four miles from his house, offered him considerable food for thought.

Whilst checking his calculations on the back of an old envelope, there came a tap on the window.

'Good evening, sir.'

'Oh, good evening, officer,' said Ralph, winding down the window and confirming – in response to the politest of enquiries – that he was, in fact, the owner of the vehicle and was, indeed, familiar with the registration number.

'Having trouble with your lights, sir?'

'Lights?' said Ralph. 'No . . . no, I don't think so. . . . Why?'

'Flashing on and off, sir. Quite spectacular at times . . . sort of son et lumière as it were.'

'Ah,' said Ralph. 'Ah, yes . . . er . . . a friend of mine, officer – fiddling with the switches.'

'You don't say, sir. And where is he now?'

'Now?' said Ralph, giving a passable imitation of the village idiot.

'That's right, sir. Now. At this moment in time, as they say.'

'He's at home.'

'Very sensible, too. Best place on a night like this, wouldn't you say, sir?'

Ralph nodded enthusiastically.

'Steering all right, is it?'

'Oh, yes. Perfect. . . . Why?'

'Swerving about, sir. . . . It's been reported that you nearly had Constable Perkins off his bicycle.'

Ralph opened his mouth to reply but, failing to pinpoint the *mot juste* as it were, he promptly closed it again.

'Let's have a look shall we, sir?' said the officer, poking his head through the window and gripping the steering wheel. His nose twitched like a bloodhound on the scent. There was a moment's pause. . . . He sniffed again. 'My word, sir. Smells like a four-ale bar in here. Been enjoying ourselves, have we?'

'No,' said Ralph quickly. 'Well, yes . . . sort of, that is. I've been playing bowls, you see and er. . . .'

'Bowls,' repeated the officer thoughtfully. 'Hmmm. . . . In the dark, sir?'

'Yes. No, er. . . . that is, not when we started.'

'I see, sir.' He pondered a moment. 'I wonder if you would mind stepping out of the vehicle for a moment.'

Out of the dark loomed another, even larger policeman, and as they flanked him on either side, knowing glances were exchanged. 'Been playing bowls, Fred,' said the first officer.

His colleague peered with exaggerated concentration into the pitch blackness and raised his eyebrows.

'Perhaps you would be kind enough to blow into this quaint little gadget, sir? . . . Won't take a moment.'

*

They were kind enough to give him a lift back from the police station and, in the true spirit of community policing, insisted on driving his car into the garage before bidding him a jovial goodnight.

Ralph braced his shoulders and inserted his key into the door. A glance at his watch informed him that he was far from out of the wood – and he was not mistaken. His lady wife shared the officers' scepticism regarding the playing of bowls in the pitch dark and the delicate matter of yet another ruined meal brought the whole sad story into the open.

But things could have been worse. Indeed – apart from the vitriolic observation that if this was what playing childish games with a lot of silly old fools led to, then the sooner he gave it up the better – he was pleasantly surprised at the mildness of the onslaught.

Our poor innocent had not the wit to perceive the devious workings of the female mind, nor to spot the delighted twinkle in her eyes at the prospect of her exclusive and unrestricted use of the car for the next twelve months.

Scarcely able to suppress a snigger, she offered a few helpful tips on how he might be able to renovate his rusty old bicycle which had been suspended from the garage roof these many years and, on the pretext of unearthing his old pair of stout walking shoes, she scuttled off to phone up all her mates, in order to formulate preliminary plans for a whole series of jolly sprees and outings during the coming year.

Our erstwhile hero, now fingerprinted and on file, slumped disconsolately in his armchair, with only the ancient Labrador for company. The poor dumb creature had not fully comprehended the finer points of the discussion, but he had gleaned enough to appreciate that there was going to be a good deal more walking in the near future than had hitherto been the case – an activity in which he was prepared to play a full and active part.

Anxious not to be found wanting when the call came, he had taken the precaution of surreptitiously fetching his lead from the kitchen and placing it beside him in his basket. Being thus equipped, he dozed off with a smile of serene contentment upon his face, to dream of happier days to come.

Ralph retired to bed to spend a restless night, haunted by visions of the steep hills which lay between him and the bowling green, and a succession of nightmares in which a certain fat little man played a prominent role.

7
Competitive Play
Club Competitions

Note: If our readers can imagine the complexities of the following chapter multiplied to cater for the machinations of the pairs, triples and fours, it is certain that they will agree that such additional complications are best postponed until they have mastered the principles of the Singles Competition.

Although it was officially too late in the season, the committee – desperately short of cash in the prize fund – saw fit to stretch a point and persuade our heroes to enter for all the Club Competitions. George was reasonably confident at his prospects, particularly with regard to the Club Championship, but Ralph would have welcomed the opportunity of holding a watching brief in his first season – getting the feel of things as it were – before taking the plunge.

Nevertheless, his experiences were to stand him in good stead for the future – and they will more than repay the careful study of our thoughtful reader.

It was not long before he reached the conclusion that the competition match – or 'comp' as it is affectionately known – falls into two separate and distinct phases:

Phase I: Before the Match (preliminary skirmishing)
Phase II: On the Green

Neither phase should be considered less important, and our reader, if keen to make his mark in the competitive field, must be at pains to attain mastery of both phases – and to note that there is more to winning competitions than the mere bowling of woods. Much can be accomplished to influence the result of the game long before the contestants take their stance upon the green.

Phase I: Before the Match

Early in the season the draw sheets are posted in the clubhouse. Inscribed upon them are the closing dates for each round, and their appearance signals the start of the ever-popular game which is played annually between those responsible for the smooth running of the competitions (hereinafter referred to as the Match Committee) and the members. Any number can play, and the rules are simple, yet the contest is utterly absorbing.

On the one hand, the committee – by pleading, bullying and threatening – attempts to get the matches played by the closing dates, while the members – slippery as a bowl of eels – pit their wits to see:

(a) by how many days they can exceed the time limit, and
(b) how many *final* warnings they can survive, before playing the tie in the nick of time to avoid disqualification.

Adherence to the rules varies from club to club – some are disposed to leniency, some are very strict, and our new bowler is advised to assess the temperature of his own particular organization.

As a general rule he should work upon the principle that what he can get away with, in terms of messing the committee about, is directly proportional to his length of membership and his position in the pecking order.

But this is not designed to discourage our aspiring bowler from participating in the excitement of the game – the occasional modest gamble is the spice of life – but he is advised to proceed with caution. As a new boy, he is just the sort of chap the committee is looking for. Should he overplay his hand, he is liable to be made an example of – kicked out of the competition as a sharp reminder to the rest of the members.

Should such drastic action be deemed necessary, our luckless novice can be assured of the moral and sympathetic support of his comrades. The popular pastime of committee-baiting for not getting the comps played off to time gives way to a groundswell of rebellious murmurings regarding the high-handed and dictatorial attitude of the officers, accompanied by threatening predictions of wholesale changes at the next AGM.

Nevertheless, it has a salutary effect upon the laggards. For a day or two the green is a bustling hive of activity, with members jostling for an empty rink on which to play their long-overdue games.

The sacrificial lamb has served his purpose, and the committee, just for the moment, holds the whip hand.

Committee holding the whip hand

Ladies Only: Our lady novice is urged to disregard much of what has been written. The iron maidens of the Ladies' Match Committee will tolerate no such impish behaviour.

To their male clubmates, the lady bowlers' ready and willing subservience to their stern, rigid and self-imposed code of conduct is a source of never-ending wonderment, and a joy to behold – particularly to their bowler husbands, whose feeble attempts to introduce a similar form of discipline into their own marital alliances have come to a very sticky end.

The Challenger

Tradition has it that the first-named player shall be deemed the challenger, and the onus is upon him to offer dates and ensure that the game is played on or before the closing date.

At club level our novice will find the lines of distinction less finely drawn, in that the role of challenger, eagerly pressing for a firm date, is usually assumed by the player who fancies his chance of winning.

In most cases, however, bearing in mind the unpredictability of the game, the likely outcome is shrouded in uncertainty, and further complicated by both parties pursuing a course of evasive action until such time as one or the other is satisfied that playing conditions are ideally suited to his particular style – or lack of it.

This, our reader will readily appreciate, all adds up to a great deal of 'jiggery-pokery' in one form or another, and turns what should be a fairly simple arrangement into a highly complex and frustrating operation.

Ralph, conscientious as ever and anxious to conform to the letter of law, was at a loss to understand the interminable shilly-shallying and piffling excuses for delaying the issue. He was even more astonished at the sudden changes of heart; the sudden urge to get the game played – strangely associated with variations in the climatic conditions.

Should our new bowler, on his first venture into the competitive field, experience similar exasperation at his inability to pin down an elusive opponent to a firm date, he may draw some small measure of comfort from the following explanation.

It may be that the green is running fast and true – admirably suited to the skilful player – in which case his less talented opponent may seek an adjournment until a day or two of torrential rain transforms the surface into a soggy quagmire, thus squaring the odds a little.

Conversely, it may be that the green is already awash and the touch player is somewhat apprehensive regarding his ability to match the brute strength of his rustic foe at hurling a cannonade of heavy woods straight up the middle.

Club members are usually divided roughly 50/50 on which way round the green plays better. Where conflicting opinions are involved, deadlock is inevitable. Others, faced with an opponent in a purple patch of brilliant form, may stall for time in the desperate hope that he will, please God, 'go off a bit'.

And of course there is always the possibility that an opponent who is: (i) a perfect gentleman (ii) going on holiday, or (iii) lacking the moral fibre for a lengthy war of attrition may get fed up with the whole miserable business and give the game. A forlorn hope, but worth a try.

Special note: Above all, it should be noted that successful evasive action enables the modest performer to drop into the general conversation a casual mention of the fact that he is still left in all the competitions. He is under no obligation to draw attention to the fact that the reason for this remarkable achievement is that, so far, no one has actually managed to make him play one.

Ralph remained puzzled, but there were no flies on George. From the outset, his beady eyes had been quick to spot the benefits which might accrue from mastering the many facets of evasive action.

He had, in fact, by delaying matters until the advent of a fierce crosswind and a surface resembling that of an underdone bread pudding, already won his first three games. Two by default and the third by virtue of the fact that his less robust opponent had failed to get a wood more than half way up the green.

Unfortunately, intoxicated with success, he had overstepped the tolerance of the Match Committee by playing the fool with their much beloved president, and had been booted out of the Championship before he had even bowled a wood.

'Oh, I can see what they're up to,' he confided in Ralph. 'Well, it's obvious, isn't it? They've got the wind up. Don't like to see a new man win it in his first year. Despicable way of going on in my view,' he snorted. And, mindful of the appalling weather forecast, he hurried off to arrange his next game to coincide with the impending deluge.

These pre-match ploys are innocent enough – enjoyed by the majority of members in a spirit of pure devilment, and spiced with the sheer bliss of being a thorn in the flesh of the committee.

But our novice is warned that, beneath the surface of this merry band, there lurks a rogue element, prepared to carry such matters to extremes in their ruthless quest for fame, and the immortality of a gold-leaf inscription on the Clubhouse Honours Board.

The Rogue Bowler

Our innocent beginner should never underestimate the menace of the RB, nor the depths of human deceit to which the miscreants will sink in order to further their ambitions. It is a mark of their cunning that they wear no badge; nor bear any distinguishing mark. To all outward appearances they are not dissimilar to any other bowler, and may easily be mistaken for the same.

Nor should our lady novice wallow in a sense of false complacency, happy in the conviction that such despicable behaviour is typical of the male sex. The lady rogue – or 'roguess' – is ever present.

(a)   (b)   (c)   (d)   (e)

Can you spot the Rogue Bowler?

Answer: (d)

But George had soon picked them out, and very impressed he had been. Here, he felt, was a group with whom he could sense an immediate affinity of spirit, and to whom he could unhesitatingly declare his allegiance.

He lost no time in obtaining a copy of their unofficial handbook, *The Rogue Bowler's Guide to Successful Match-play* by I. Cheetham and, without delay, applied himself to a crash-course of serious study.

Note: Excerpts from George's copy of the handbook will be quoted throughout this chapter, in the hope that the startling revelations contained therein will serve as a timely warning of the snares and pitfalls that await the unwary novice.

But dear Ralph, still harbouring a pathetic faith in the basic goodness of his fellow man, once again failed to spot the danger signals. It was therefore inevitable that the mischievous hand of Fate should decree that, of our two heroes, he should be the first to face the ultimate test, in the shape of a certain Mr Harold Tutt, generally acknowledged as one of the most accomplished 'rogues' ever to grace the portals of the Highcliffe Bowling Club.

As challenger, Ralph dutifully offered a selection of possible dates but, for one reason or another, certain difficulties prevailed. It was not that Mr Tutt was unable to be at the club; in fact he was there all the time. To tell the truth, our hero sensed that his current form was under the closest scrutiny – and in all due modesty he had to admit that he was bowling extremely well.

'He's keeping an eye on you,' chuckled the Hon.Sec.

Ralph was mildly amused at the suggestion . . . the poor chap actually thought the Hon.Sec. might be speaking in jest.

Ralph tried again, and to be fair, his opponent could not have been more co-operative. Why, on no less than three occasions a firm date was agreed and a marker arranged, only for Harold to fall victim to yet another diabolical misfortune which necessitated a further postponement.

The first was a severely sprained thumb, as the result of an encounter with a particularly stubborn jar of pickled onions; the second as a result of contracting the virulent twenty-four-hour virus – which appears without warning and disappears without trace – commonly known as 'Rogue's Flu'.

George might have allowed his friend a peek at his copy of the Rogue's handbook – especially page 26 headed:

Evasive Action for the Rogue Bowler

To be employed on all occasions when the weather, the green or the excellent form of your opponent gives cause for concern.

(a) *Injury or Affliction*

A tried and trusted favourite, offering countless possibilities for combination and permutation, and scope for original ideas. Renders all Match Committees powerless. Suspicious, yes, but powerless.

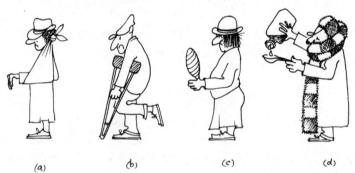

(a)   (b)   (c)   (d)

Rogue Bowlers arriving to play match, in conditions not to their liking

Notes

(i) Restrict to strains, sprains and pains. Avoid flesh wounds or lacerations. Conditions may alter and the visual evidence of scar tissue may prove an embarrassment to the RB wishing to play within the hour.

(ii) Check that in (c) the bandaged thumb is on the bowling hand.

(iii) The addition of the pathetically murmured phrase: 'I'm afraid I'll just have to give you the game,' adds a nice touch. Instantly arouses the sympathy of bystanders, and places your opponent in an invidious position.

Caution: Beware of seasoned campaigner likely to retort:

'Thank you very much. I'll take it,' and, with a swift flourish of his pen, strike your name from the list.

On the occasion of the third attempt to play the game, our hero had actually changed and was ready to set foot upon the green when the clubhouse telephone rang. Harold was abject in his apologies, but even Ralph was hard put to suppress un-Christian thoughts. Not that he would dream of doubting the word of a fellow bowler, but there could not be many households suffering the misfortune of a burst pipe while the rest of the country sweltered in the midst of an August heatwave.

Rogue Bowler apologizing for late cry-off, owing to domestic crisis

The late cry-off is a favourite ploy of the RB and the relevant excerpt from the Rogue's handbook may be of service to our reader.

Last Minute Cry-offs — use with discretion. Emergencies only. Telephone or messenger – avoid direct eyeball contact.

(i) Household Crisis:	burst pipe, gasman, washing machine, bailiffs or rodent inspector, etc.
(ii) Car Breakdown:	puncture, clutch, gearbox, battery, water pump or, for the technically minded rogue, the half shaft lock nut sprocket spline retaining pin, etc.
(iii) Bereavement:	greengrocer's second cousin, budgerigar, cat, hamster, tortoise, etc.

The thoughtful rogue is advised to keep meticulous notes of the examples employed, in order to avoid undue repetition. The failure of your fourth gearbox in the last six weeks, or the untimely demise of yet another cat may arouse unwelcome suspicion and severely damage your credibility rating.

Ralph was disappointed. . . . And so was George. Day after day the sun shone down from a clear blue sky. Day after day he scanned the distant horizon, hoping for a glimpse of a looming thundercloud . . . but not a sign.

There seemed to be no end to this interminable spell of fine weather and, having no intention of chancing his arm in conditions ideally suited to his skilful opponent, he turned for inspiration to his copy of the handbook.

Having exhausted the standard procedures he felt the need to come up with something rather special, and speedily thumbed his way to the more advanced examples.

'Ahaa!' he cried. 'And what have we here, I ask myself,' he gloated, stubbing a podgy forefinger at the heading '*The Thespian Ploy – Advanced Rogues only. (Preferably with some experience in Amateur Theatricals.)*'

As per instructions George arrived at the clubhouse in a mood of enthusiastic anticipation, well before the appointed hour – in fact, a whole twenty-four hours before the appointed hour. Taking care that the procedure was well observed, he completed the preliminaries with a flourish. He polished his woods; made out the score card; took out the mats and the jack – and set up the scoreboard on the bank.

All preparations completed, he took up his position on the green and, after several ostentatious examinations of his watch, began to demand in a loud and penetrating voice some information regarding the whereabouts of his opponent. 'Where the devil has the fellow got to? . . . Can't hang about here all night, you know. . . . Anybody seen him?'

Having by this means established the general situation, he accosted two inoffensive committee members who were rolling up on the next rink, and proceeded to give them a sound ticking off on the subject of their incompetence in getting the club comps played off on time.

'Now look here, you chaps. It's not good enough, you know.'

Conditioned by many years of service to being the butt and target of general abuse, the browbeaten members hung their heads in shame, and our chubby rogue pressed home his advantage.

'No point in you fellows making all these rules and regulations about the comps, if you don't keep the members up to the mark.'

Then, grudgingly accepting their apologies for any inconvenience that he had suffered, and assurances that the matter would be duly investigated, George collected up the equipment and left the premises in a regal huff.

Closing the gate behind him, he could not help but chuckle as he recalled the closing paragraph from the handbook.

. . . The ensuing smokescreen of counter-accusation and denial should drive the committee into a rare tizzy, and the resulting confusion should grant you a further few days' grace, by which time the weather may have deteriorated sufficiently to favour your more agricultural style of bowling.

In all modesty, he felt that he had carried off the ruse with considerable aplomb. Was there, he wondered, such an award as a Rogue 'Oscar' – if so, he felt he must be in with a chance.

He stepped jauntily along the path and, once out of sight of the clubhouse, he gave vent to his exuberance with a tiny skip of delight.

George's problem was temporarily resolved, but Ralph was not happy. No sooner had the matter of the burst pipe been overcome than Harold developed a decided limp, and our hero, convinced that an early confrontation was out of the question, rather lost interest, and with it, sad to say, his concentration.

For some time now his good lady had been agitating on the subject of completing the patio wall which had been started well before the season. Reflecting that the next few days might offer the opportunity of pouring a little oil on the marital waters, he succumbed to the pressures, and placed an order for the sand and cement.

The trap was sprung. Like so many innocents before him he had dropped his guard at the crucial moment, and his rogue opponent, seizing the opportunity for which he had been so patiently waiting, lost no time in administering the dreaded 'Sting'.

Note: Readers unfamiliar with this slangy expression from the era of Al Capone and his Chicago hoodlums will find it clearly defined on page 57 of the Rogue's handbook.

The Sting

. . . Whilst skilfully manipulating the subtle nuances of delaying tactics, the true rogue will never lose sight of the main objective, i.e., spotting the critical moment to administer the *coup de grace* or 'Sting'. He must be ever vigilant – ready to pounce as soon as the fickle wheel of fortune spins the odds in his favour. A missed opportunity is lost and gone for ever, and so he must keep his adversary under strict surveillance, pressing for the game to be played upon the instant that his unwary opponent is observed to be at some temporary disadvantage, such as:

(a) starting a beastly cold
(b) preoccupied with anxiety regarding imminent appointment with: bank manager, income tax man or stipendiary magistrate
(c) nursing septic finger
(d) in throes of domestic upheaval, in that his dear wife has left him – even more traumatic in that his dear wife has come back
(e) thoughtlessly undertaking mammoth DIY project, involving severe muscular strain certain to destroy his delicate sense of touch

Pausing awhile in the midst of his third mix, Ralph gently eased his protesting back muscles into a semi-upright posture and gave vent to a low moan. Panting and gasping in the throes of a severe oxygen deficiency, he slumped upon his shovel and wiped the stinging perspiration from his eyes . . . when he was suddenly aware of a figure leaning nonchalantly over the fence, watching the proceedings with a thoughtful look.

'How do?' said Harold chirpily.

Rogue Bowler keeping opponent under strict surveillance

'All fixed for tonight,' said Harold brightly. 'Only one rink left, so I've booked it. Sid says he'll mark for us.'

Ralph opened his mouth to reply, but nothing came out – although his desperate efforts to catch his breath could have been mistaken for a nod of assent.

'Half past five to six?' said Harold considerately. 'Well, say six o'clock shall we? See you later then.' And off he went.

Our hero stumbled to the fence and pawed the air in a feeble attempt to recall him. . . . Harold looked back and returned a friendly wave as he rounded the corner and disappeared.

As he sat on his locker that evening, gently massaging his stiffening thigh muscles, Ralph could not help feeling that things had not gone entirely the way he had envisaged.

Harold, in the true rogue tradition of keeping one's opponent kicking his heels, arrived at twenty past six and, beginning as ever with the spoken word, embarked without delay upon the softening-up process.

Whilst changing his shoes and polishing his woods, the experienced rogue establishes beyond all doubt that:

(a) he is not bowling well himself – right off form
(b) only hopes that he will be able to make a game of it – at least put up some sort of show
(c) he is not really interested in competitive play – much prefers a nice friendly roll-up, and only enters the comps to support the club as a dutiful member should

By the time Harold had finished, Ralph was not only feeling guilty at having harried such a nice unassuming chap into playing at all, but decidedly uneasy at being the hot favourite, expected to win quite comfortably in the face of such poor-quality opposition.

'Do you like to chat?' enquired Harold politely. 'Or would you prefer to concentrate? . . . It doesn't matter to me. It's entirely up to you, old man.'

Ralph scratched his chin. He did not really like too much talking, but on the other hand he did not wish to appear unsociable. 'Well, I er . . .' he mumbled. It was a ticklish situation.

Our reader is advised not to waste his time on such fruitless speculation, as the following excerpt from the handbook will reveal:

. . . Having ascertained that your opponent is quite happy to chat, lapse into a glum and oppressive silence. If silent concentration is his preference, maintain a ceaseless prattle of wearisome small talk.

With the softening-up process duly completed, all was now ready for the game to start. Harold rose to his feet and sighed. 'Might as well get it over and done with, I suppose. . . . It shouldn't take too long, I'm afraid,' he added sadly, and limped painfully out of the changing room.

Phase II: On the Green

The Rogue Bowler is aware that, no matter how shrewdly he has manipulated the pre-match procedure, it is here, on the green, that his prowess will be put to the ultimate test.

The Trial Ends

Whilst taking careful note of the line and pace of the green by the closest scrutiny of Ralph's woods, Harold confirmed his previous claims of being right off form by bowling so badly that it was embarrassing. Ralph did so hope that he would improve. After all, he didn't want to win too easily and, to set his opponent at his ease, he offered a few words of comfort and reassurance.

Harold thanked him with a shy smile, and promptly delivered a 'wrong bias'. 'Oh, dear. There, I've done it again,' he wailed. . . . 'I say, Ralph. I hope you don't mind my asking – it is the small ring on the outside, isn't it?'

He listened attentively with wide-eyed innocence as our hero patiently demonstrated which way round to hold the bowl. His gratitude was most touching.

Our reader must be saddened to observe how, even before the game had started, Ralph was basking in a warm glow of complacency, and already turning his thoughts to the subject of whom he would be playing in the next round.

Tutty, well pleased with the way things were going, turned his attention to confirming his claims of total disinterest by needing to be reminded every time that it was his turn to bowl, whose woods were which and where, and generally displaying a bird-brained inability to keep his mind on the game for two minutes together. . . . 'I see they've repainted the lavatory door,' he observed, at a critical moment when Ralph was lying three shots. 'I must say I don't care much for the colour. . . . Oh, er . . . is it my turn now?'

Ralph could not suppress a smirk. Alas! His attitude might have been less condescending had he been familiar with the following excerpt from page 63 of the handbook:

. . . Having taken careful note of the exact disposition of the woods, peer about vacantly and attract your opponent's attention to the presence of a Lesser Spotted Wagtail in a nearby tree . . .

. . . Wax lyrical on the richness and beauty of its plumage, thus establishing the relative unimportance of a silly little game of bowls when viewed in the context of the Grand Order of Nature.

This should convince your opponent that he is up against nothing more than a prize buffoon.

While he is still smirking, draw the shot.

But in this case, Tutty's cunning ruse proved counterproductive, serving merely to jolt our hero from his complacency and re-awaken him to the dangers of underestimating one's opponent. He buckled to his task and, despite the crippling after-effects of shovelling a small hillock of sand, he began to bowl quite well. So well, in fact, that Harold was obliged to introduce additional measures and augment the spoken word with some delightful aspects of positional play.

Note: In view of the subsequent havoc wrought upon our hero's length and line, it is imperative to acquaint our reader with the relevant section from the RB's handbook.

Page 67
... No true rogue will run the risk of exposure by committing a flagrant breach of the Law requiring him to remain behind the mat while his opponent is in possession.

Nevertheless, by taking up a strategic position on the wing, it is still possible for him to exert his influence on the state of play.

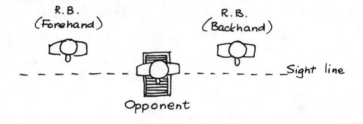

He should note that, by inclining the head and trunk to an angle of 45°, he can intrude into his opponent's field of vision, whilst keeping his feet behind the mat and within the letter of the Law.

Your sudden appearance, at the precise moment of delivery, will prove a highly effective distraction.

But all rogues are advised to be on the alert, and ready to sprint to the opposite wing should a desperate opponent change his hand in an attempt to erase you from his field of vision. It is well worth the extra effort.

Your opponent will be so anxious to get the bowl away before you 'pop up' again, that his thoughtful assessment of line and length will be adversely affected by undue haste.

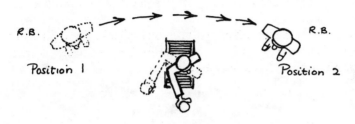

Position 1   Position 2

Musical Version

The addition of a little light music adds a subtle refinement to all aspects of positional play, and has enabled many an RB to recover from a seemingly hopeless position. Loud melodic whistling is detectable from the bank and should be avoided. As a general rule, members should aim at a slightly off-key hissing through clenched teeth — something akin to a simmering kettle with an ill-fitting lid.

Musical tastes vary, but the rhythmic beat of Ravel's *Bolero* has a proven success record, and many senior rogues will recall the occasion when their much respected president pulled back to win from 18:4 down with a spirited selection from *The Mikado*.

By a superhuman effort of concentration – and a stubborn refusal to bowl until Harold was well back behind the mat – our hero managed to keep in touch. But, unfortunately for him, it was a glorious summer's evening and the lengthening shadows at the pavilion end gave Tutty the chance to introduce one of the most formidable weapons in the armoury of the Rogue Bowler:

Shadow Play – in which the exponent positions himself to ensure that his shadow falls directly across his opponent's line of sight.

Ralph thought at first that it was but a passing cloud, and was not unduly perturbed. Disappointed, but undaunted, Harold promptly introduced a series of sudden jerky movements culminating in the remedial exercises for a stiff bowling arm, as laid down on page 77 of the handbook.

... vigorous arm circling exercises to loosen the shoulder muscles creates a flickering strobe effect, most disconcerting to the man on the mat . . .

... should your opponent glare round and catch you in the act, switch to pretence of swatting imaginary wasp or adjusting stubborn buckle at the back of twisted braces.

Harold was pulling ahead now. By dint of some excellent shadow work he had established a lead of some half a dozen shots but, having been caught red-handed, he sought to consolidate his lead by tactical switch to the more demanding realms of:

Shadow Sculpture (page 79)

... Our artistic rogue, having dissipated his entire school life in the projection of assorted animal heads on the classroom wall, may wish to re-coup some of those wasted years by directing his talents to the projection of various life forms on to the green in front of his opponent.

Chosen subjects are a matter of personal preference and individual ability. The gorilla, orang-utan and the Abominable Snowman have been used to good effect, while one redoubtable RB has achieved a remarkable success rate with his celebrated version of:

The Hunchback of Notre Dame

Harold was no mean performer, and although his version contained some slight imperfections, the surprise element cost Ralph a further two shots on that end. Two shots that might well have been saved had he been familiar with the warning on page 80 of the handbook.

Cautionary Note (Artistic Rogues)

. . . Before employing any form of shadow sculpture weigh up the quality of your opposition. Beware of seasoned campaigner likely to nullify your celebrated 'Hunchback' with the crushing riposte:

'Very good – one of my favourite books. And now, as an encore, perhaps you might care to concentrate on your version of "The Invisible Man" . . .'

George had long since classified Harold as an out-and-out rogue and, eager to pick up a few useful pointers to improve his own technique, he had made a special point of giving this game his undivided attention.

He had been so impressed, particularly with this latest manoeuvre, that he retired, without delay, to a secluded spot behind the clubhouse to try out this shadow sculpture business for himself.

Unfortunately, his physical limitations imposed certain restrictions upon the imaginative quality of his work. No matter how hard he tried to project an image of grotesque and terrifying proportions, the end result was always a sort of amiable 'Humpty-Dumpty!' . . . He was mortified.

Ralph was struggling now. He could feel the game slipping away, and was relieved to get to the other end where, with the sun in their faces, he could at least enjoy a temporary respite from the unrelenting shadows.

But his optimism was ill-founded. Operating for most of the time under the lowering skies and scudding clouds of the Great British Summer, it would be a foolish Rogue, indeed, who pinned his faith to a clear blue sky and ignored the merits of the less spectacular, but equally effective –

Noises Off (Sound Only)

Ralph was poised at the crucial point of his backswing when the rattle and clatter shattered the silence. The convulsive jerk of his arm projected his bowl way beyond the jack, and way off line to boot. On his next delivery it came again. Puzzled, and not a little vexed, he looked round. But he could see nothing untoward. Only his opponent, innocently admiring the splendour of the distant clouds, forming up for what promised to be a glorious sunset.

When next it was his turn he waited, poised upon the mat ... nothing. He looked round suspiciously – then, before it should come again, launched his bowl in such haste that the result was equally disastrous.

Poor Ralph was not sure which was worse – the sudden noise or the waiting. The tense silence, the uncertainty. ... But he caught him in the end, spinning round in the nick of time to catch his tormenter aiming a swift kick at the waiting bowls, which rattled about like a line of goods trucks in a shunting yard.

Harold smiled ingratiatingly. 'Mind you don't step back on these, old chap,' he said solicitously. 'You could easily sprain your ankle, you know.'

Thus forewarned, our reader should be able to cope with any artificially created noise. But, within the confines of socially acceptable behaviour, no effective advice can be offered to the beginner confronted by the Rogue Bowler blessed with certain physical abnormalities.

Short of stooping to offensive remarks of a highly personal nature, there is little that can be done to prevent the accomplished Rogue taking full advantage of ill-fitting dentures or double-jointed knuckles.

But Ralph was now a changed man. His faith in the basic goodness of mankind, if not shattered, was definitely blunted. Incensed at his discovery of a fellow bowler engaging in a blatant act of sharp practice revived the fighting spirit of his youth. With jutting jaw and lips set in a line of grim determination, he shut eyes and ears to all distractions, and fought back to level the scores at 14–14.

Tutty sighed, and shook his head sadly. 'Oh, dear,' he mused. 'It did seem a shame. After all, the chap was only a beginner.'

But our Rogue was desperate. This was the only comp he was left in. His last hope for this season. . . . 'Ah, well,' he reflected. 'All's fair in love and war, I suppose . . . and the Claude Ball Consolation Handicap.'

He watched dispassionately as Ralph put up the jack and drew a beautiful first wood. Right on it. But not touching. Perfect – just about an inch in front.

Harold sighed again. He realized that the time had come to dispense with the niceties of the subtle approach. The lad was displaying a particularly stubborn streak, and there was nothing for it but to play the Rogue Bowler's trump card. . . .

The Direct Frontal Approach

'I hope you don't mind,' said Harold innocently, 'but what an unusual grip you have, Ralph. I must say it certainly works for you. Would you mind if I copied it?'

Ralph flushed just a trifle. He was only too pleased to demonstrate.

'Hmmm,' said Harold, carefully arranging his fingers around our hero's bowl. 'Most interesting – probably accounts for the smoothness of your delivery. We were discussing your perfect action only the other day – right out of the text book. Yes, most interesting. . . . Oh, I am sorry,' he said, handing back the bowl. 'It's your turn, isn't it.'

Conscious of the admiring scrutiny of his pupil, Ralph concentrated on achieving pure elegance of style.

Harold gasped in wonderment. 'Beautiful,' he murmured. 'Quite beautiful. Pretty to watch.'

Ralph could not resist the tiniest glow of pride, ignoring for the moment that his flowery follow through had projected the bowl some three yards past the jack.

'And you've shortened your backswing, haven't you? I must certainly try that.'

'Have I?' said Ralph.

'Oh, yes. Most definitely,' said Harold, stepping onto the mat.

Our hero pondered on this. He retired to the bank and checked it out with a few practice swings, neglecting to observe that, in the meantime, his opponent was gently edging his wood off the jack.

'And that little turn of the wrist, just before you release the bowl. . . . Is that your own idea, or did you get it from the book?'

Ralph scratched his head. 'Well I er . . . Do you know, I've never really thought about it.' He scratched his head again, and peered hard at his wrist.

'But look here,' said Harold, consumed with remorse, 'I'm awfully sorry, old man. I'm taking your mind off your game.'

Tutty had a whole string of further observations up his sleeve regarding his opponent's style and technique but, as things turned out, they proved unnecessary. The seeds of critical self-analysis had been sown, and from now on it was all downhill for our hero.

Preoccupied with the business of checking and rechecking his grip and the length of his backswing – and twiddling his wrist around until it was quite painful – he proceeded to spray his woods to all parts of the rink.

Harold trundled his bowls somewhere in the region of the jack, and in a couple of ends it was all over.

'Shake hands,' said the marker.

Ralph stood bemused. Eyes glazed and mouth slightly open, in a state of mild shock at the swiftness of his execution.

'Bad luck, old man,' said Harold, turning to our hero with outstretched hand. 'Just not your day, was it – but thanks for the game.'

'Oh, yes and er . . . thank you,' said Ralph. As well he might. It had been a lesson from which he would profit for the rest of his bowling days.

Postscript

George had observed his fellow Rogue's performance with a measure of admiration bordering on hero-worship and, mindful of his forthcoming encounter with Herbert, he hurried home to brush up on one or two points in the handbook.

Thus equipped, he strode down to the club the following day whistling the stirring theme of the 'Dam Busters' which reflected his mood of supreme confidence.

Throughout the preliminaries and the trial ends everything went according to plan, and George was well pleased. He had little doubt regarding the outcome of this trifling encounter.

But halfway through the first end proper, things took a turn for the worse. . . .

Herbert paused for a moment with his wood held at arm's length, then dropped it onto the mat with a sickening thud.

'Oi!' he said quietly, and gently taking the knot of our chubby hero's tie between his finger and thumb, as if to make a minor adjustment, he drew him into such close proximity that their noses were barely an inch apart. . . .

'Now,' said Herbert, in a soft murmur edged with menace, 'get yourself behind the mat ... over there, with your shadow off the rink. . . . *And*,' he added, tightening the knot so that George's eyes fairly boggled from their sockets, 'you can cut out that damn fool whistling when I'm on the mat. Right?'

George nodded eagerly and retired to the bank in some haste, from where, as he struggled to loosen the iron-hard knot which was crushing his Adam's apple, he glowered sulkily at the sea of grinning faces in the clubhouse window.

Needless to say, he was soon on the receiving end of a thorough lesson in the art of bowls, and a sound thrashing. From which he – and, we trust, our thoughtful readers – will profit for the rest of their bowling days.

8
The Marker

The singles player, striving to attain perfect co-ordination twixt hand and eye, is at the same time engaged in a relentless struggle to formulate a strategy that will outwit his wily foe.

Innumerable problems beset him on every side; encompassing immaculate drawing to the jack; removing opponent's bowls; the pinpoint accuracy of positional woods – and a vigilant eye for the menace of back bowls.

All these, however, pale into insignificance compared to the problem of enlisting the services of a good marker, or any marker at all, come to that.

It is a mark of the unfairness of human society that – in addition to cornering an elusive opponent – the luckless challenger is also held responsible for securing a marker.

Right from the start our aspiring bowler should note that evasive action is not confined to the competitor. The extensive range of excuses for not being able to play is exceeded only by the astonishing variety of imaginative reasons for not being able to mark. And our novice is warned that the direct approach, in the form of a general enquiry, is utterly useless.

Inexperienced bowler: 'Anyone care to mark a game?'

Until he has mastered the subtleties of marker recruitment, the new bowler is advised to make a start by getting a few 'in the bank' as it were. As an insurance against future requirements, he should volunteer to mark for an assortment of players – thus establishing a pool of members under the statutory obligation of repaying the favour on a 'knock-for-knock' basis.

A sense of obligation can also be nurtured by chauffering, lawn cutting or a promise of your wholehearted support for his bid to get on the committee at the next AGM.

For the lazy novice, bribery – in the form of garden produce, alcohol or tobacco – is a feasible proposition. While, for the ruthless opportunist, should the occasion arise, a mild form of blackmail is not to be spurned.

Note: With the mellowing effects of the passing years, such opportunities are regrettably rare. But they do occur.

One Highcliffe couple have been fortunate enough to secure the services of regular markers by the chance discovery of a minor indiscretion on the part of a happily married member and the Hon. Treasurer of the Ladies' Section.

Keen singles bowler securing services of a regular marker

The preceding suggestions, though perfectly adequate for the beginner, do entail some measure of effort and/or financial outlay, and the majority of experienced bowlers prefer, as always, to nail their colours to the mast of the spoken word based on individual contact.

But, as with the general enquiry, the direct approach is equally useless: e.g. '*Will you mark for me next Tuesday at 6 o'clock?*' – WRONG!!!

The intended victim, appraised of the exact time and date has the relatively simple task of claiming a prior engagement, and all is lost.

The correct spoken word procedure is best illustrated in theatrical form, and the dramatic work which follows illustrates a typical scenario which may be observed – with minor variations – in any clubhouse on most evenings throughout the season.

The work was first presented by the Dramatic Section of the Lower Piddling BC at the Annual Dinner of the Rogue Bowlers' Assoc.

For the benefit of those readers who were not privileged to be present, we reproduce the complete text together with production notes based on the first, and, quite possibly, the only performance.

'It moved me.' Drama critic – *Piddling Echo*

'Nor did he return.' Chairman–Piddling Thespians DS

MARK - ANTHONY

A DRAMA

Scene: A Bowling Club's Clubhouse
Time: The present

Characters in the play:

Edward Hunter: A competitor in search of a marker
Anthony Quarry: An innocent
Barman: Non-speaking

(*As the scene opens,* Hunter *is discovered draped nonchalantly against the bar, sipping a glass of the club's indifferent cooking bitter. He is in pensive mood. From offstage L. come sounds of unrest and voices raised in anger . . . There is a long pause . . . not entirely for dramatic effect – largely because the Stage Manager has mislaid a vital moustache . . .*

Hunter *glances anxiously at the door, shuffles uncomfortably and takes another gulp . . . Without warning the door L. is flung open and* Anthony Quarry *is propelled violently onto the stage.*

He is a tall dark man, wearing a club tie and supporting with his forefinger a hastily gummed ginger moustache, sadly the only example the harassed Stage Manager could locate in the emergency . . .

He drifts unsuspectingly towards the bar.

The barman – *an inexperienced young fellow, unwillingly coerced into deputizing for his uncle who is playing in the Double Fours – stares at the approaching figure and collapses into a fit of the giggles* . . .

Hunter: (*glaring furiously at* Quarry) My dear chap. How nice to see you. What will you have?

Quarry: Nthat's nthvery kineth of nthew . . . perthnaps njust a thnalf.

Hunter: You what? . . . (*he cuffs* Quarry's *hand from his nose*) What was that you said?

Quarry: Eh? . . . Oh, er . . . That's very kind of you – perhaps just a half.

Hunter: (*grandly*) A *pint* of bitter for my friend, if you please, my good man.

(Barman *indulges in lengthy rigmarole of obsequious bowing and forelock tugging.* Hunter *fixes him with an icy stare*)

Quarry: Oh, really you shouldn't . . .

(*aside to audience*) Stap me vitals! A pint forsooth . . . 'Tis strange – something is afoot . . .

(*to* Hunter) But thanks awfully, just the same.

Hunter: Not at all, old man, My pleasure . . . (*aside*) 'Tis well begun. One slip and he is mine . . .

(*They quaff their ale*)

Oh by the way, Anthony – are you doing anything special next week?

(No reply . . . Hunter *glowers angrily at* Quarry *who is, in turn, staring mesmerized at the ginger moustache, now floating on top of his beer.* Barman *sinks from sight below the counter to roll about in helpless laughter* . . . Quarry *grins sheepishly at* Hunter *who plucks the offending object from the glass and hurls it behind the bar* . . .)

Hunter: (*through gritted teeth*) As I was saying . . . Oh by the way, Anthony – are you doing anything special next week?

Quarry: (*pulling himself together*) Well, I er . . . that is, er . . . possibly not all the week. . . . (*aside*) What means he thus? Do I perceive some hint of knavish treachery? . . . I will have none of it. . . . But stay. What if I should miss the chance of some small thing that would delight me? . . . Some morsel that would to my advantage be . . . I would hear more. (*to* Hunter) What er . . . had you in er . . . mind, as it were?

Hunter: (*aside*) Aha! The fish comes nigh the hook. . . . (*to* Quarry) Oh, I just wondered if you might do me a favour, old man?

Quarry: (*aside*) Fie! 'Twas as I did suspect . . . . What is this favour? I like it not. Yet I cannot refuse him out of hand while yet I sup his ale.

Hunter: (*aside*) See how he strains upon the rack of doubt. . . . He likes it not. Yet he cannot refuse me out of hand while yet he sups my ale.

(Barman *rises slowly from behind counter, grinning foolishly and now sporting a large ginger moustache*)

Quarry: A favour, you say? . . . Well, naturally – if I can, that is. . . . Yes, only too pleased.

Hunter: (*aside to audience*) Gadzooks! I have him now. . . .
(*aside to* Barman) Get that damned thing off!
(*aside to audience*) Now is the moment. . . . Now will I strike.
(*to* Quarry) Would you care to mark a game for me?

Quarry: (*aside*) Viper! Alas, that it should come to this. . . . And still no word of time nor place. I am undone. . . . But soft . . . although but faint there doth remain one slender chance. . . .
(*to* Hunter) Well, I er . . . I might be able to. . . . When er . . . What I mean is er . . . Which evening had you in . . . er mind?

Hunter: (*aside*) Ho, foolish wretch! That he should think to be acquainted with such news. . . . Now to tease the wriggling fish into the net. . . . (Hunter *lays a kindly hand on* Quarry's *shoulder*) Look here, old man. I don't want to put you out. . . . Let's put it like this – what night *can't* you make?

Quarry: (*aside*) Oh, woe! I fear that all is lost. The trap doth clench its hideous fangs. He hath me by the anatomies. . . . But courage. Stiffen the sinews . . .
I will my all stake on
One last despairing throw . . .
(*to* Hunter) er, not Tuesday, old chap. Definitely can't make Thursday . . . and er . . . Friday could be a problem.

Hunter: (*aside*) Ha! Ha! 'Tis done. The die is cast. . . .
(*to* Quarry) Splendid! You're OK for Wednesday then? Thanks a lot, old man. I'll just put it in the diary.

(Quarry *exits L.... a sad dejected figure* ... Hunter *reaches for the telephone*)
Oh, Harry. We'll have to change it to Wednesday, I'm afraid. ... Yes, it's the only night I can get a marker. OK? ... Oh, good.
(*He replaces the receiver ... a flicker of a smile hovers on his lips as he takes a gleaming gold-topped fountain pen from his breast pocket and – with a flamboyant gesture – flings open the diary ...*)

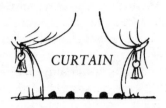

CURTAIN

By tradition, the novice is allowed the same rights as the next man in the field of marking evasion, but – once engaged – he should perform the task to the very best of his ability. Nothing condemns a bowler in the eyes of his fellows – particularly the artful dodgers – as much as a display of poor marking.

If you cannot wriggle out of the job, then be a good marker. And to be a good marker, our reader should be aware of the requirements – which are, in truth, very few. By Law, he is required to ensure that the jack is within the legal limits; answer when questioned; measure when requested and generally keep out of the way – and keep quiet.

The highest accolade that a marker can receive is that, at the end of the game, no one can remember his name, or whether there had been a marker at all.

The Rogue Marker

We shall leave aside, for the moment, the occasional black sheep who deliberately performs the task as badly as possible, in order to avoid being asked again.

Such behaviour is not only utterly reprehensible, but ill conceived. Should any undesirable elements among our readers find this devious little scheme appealing to their baser instincts, they are warned that – with demand constantly outstripping supply – such gross conduct is no guarantee of immunity.

'After all, a bad marker is better than no marker at all,' was a remark often heard from the window seat of the Highcliffe clubhouse.

It was a view that was to be somewhat modified in the light of subsequent events. ...

George's ambition to establish himself as a successful Rogue Bowler had – you will recall – been nipped in the bud at a very early stage. As a result, obliged to rely solely on his own natural bowling ability, his participation in the club comps also came to a speedy conclusion, and he found himself at something of a loose end.

Had he not, as he put it, 'reached his peak', he might have taken the opportunity of a few practice sessions, but the idea did not appeal and he preferred to cast around for a while in search of inspiration.

Whilst thus engaged, his critical eye embraced further encounters in the club comps, and he was forced to the conclusion that the standard of marking left much to be desired. He was, quite frankly, appalled at the lax and permissive approach of the presiding officials, and the manner in which they failed to stamp their personalities and authority on the matches under their jurisdiction.

Now here, George felt, was an area in which he could truly make his mark. Freed, temporarily, from the burden of competitive play, he would take this opportunity of making a worthwhile contribution to the general tone of the club, by setting an example that would raise the overall standard of marking to an acceptable level.

Within forty-eight hours of his momentous decision, two doughty adversaries – in the shape of Arnold Pratt and dear old Ralph – strode from the clubhouse to engage in combat. Strode is perhaps not quite the word. Arnold, to be fair – in view of the slight chill in the air – was executing little more than a reluctant shuffle. Indeed, only the impatient captain's threat of instant disqualification had eased him through the doorway.

He peered around. Although cast in the role of challenger, he had made no attempt to arrange a marker and, with no likely candidate in sight, he was still cherishing the faint hope of an eleventh-hour reprieve, when the window was flung open: 'I say, you chaps looking for a marker?' said George.

Ralph winced. Arnold scowled and hesitated for a moment, then perceiving the captain's beady eye upon him, gave a resigned nod.

'Now, which rink do you want?' said George. 'Personally I've always found No. 3 very good – right in front of the window.'

Our two gladiators had envisaged a more unobtrusive trundle on the end rink but, before they could demur, George had bustled off to address himself to the old boys rolling up on Rink 3.

'Come along, you chaps,' he said, snapping his fingers brusquely. 'You'll have to move, I'm afraid. Competition on here.'

Old Tom removed his pipe and cast a thoughtful eye along the other five empty rinks. 'Get stuffed,' he said, without undue emphasis, and replaced his pipe.

'On second thoughts,' said George, returning to his charges, 'we'll take Rink 4. One or two nasty patches on No. 3. Wouldn't be fair to either of you. . . . Come along, then. Let's get started. No need to bother with trial ends – I've always found them a waste of time, you know.'

Ralph was agreeable – anything for a quiet life. But Arnold was not to be deprived of his rights, and expressed this view in no uncertain terms.

'Hmmmm,' muttered George, as he grudgingly centred the jack for the first trial end. 'Fellow's going to be troublesome, I can see. Needs taking down a peg or two. . . .' and, without so much as a word, promptly kicked all Arnold's trial woods into the ditch, underlining his displeasure by imparting a fund of detailed information regarding the bowls of his friend.

Needless to say, the genial conviviality of the occasion was not helped by this display of petulance; nor was the shining hour improved by the conclusion of the first end proper. As soon as the last bowl came to rest, George broke up the head with a good swift kick and marched off to the other end.

'Two to Ralph,' he chirped, as they crossed.

'Two?' said Arnold, scowling. 'Are you sure? I would have liked a look at my last bowl.'

George drew himself up. 'Really?' he said haughtily. 'I can't think why. Personally, I should have been thoroughly ashamed of it.'

The game continued, and whatever criticism might be levelled at our marker, lack of interest could not be included. Indeed, it was not long before Arnold became gruffly outspoken on the subject of our hero leaping into the head after every delivery, in order to re-assess the position.

'Look at him now,' he wailed to the panel of experts in the window. 'It's the same every time. Whenever I get on the mat, I can't see a thing for his great fat backside.'

'You could be two down. Might be three,' announced our hero, emerging ruddy of face and perspiring freely from his exertions. 'I should draw to save if I were you.'

'Thank you. Most kind,' said Arnold, rather nastily. 'I had considered following a similar course of action, once you get out of the way. . . . Do you mind keeping right out of the head until we ask,' he snarled.

George retired to the bank in a huff. 'Ungrateful swine,' he muttered. 'That's the last time I shall put myself out to give him the benefit of my advice.'

Ruffled and aggrieved by this slight contretemps, Arnold delivered what can only be described as an irritable little bowl. The little beast hissed through the head, missing everything by the merest hair's-breadth.

George sniggered vindictively – and very loudly. 'No change, Ralph, old chap,' he called reassuringly.

With a good yard to play with Ralph drew another, and George was moved to a round of spontaneous applause. 'Oh, well bowled, sir,' he cried. 'Four to Ralph.'

But Arnold had arrived hot foot, and was having none of it. 'Just a minute. I'll have that measured,' he growled, indicating his nearest wood.

George raised his eyes to heaven – implying that a visit to the local optician's might not be out of place – then, nonchalantly applying the measure to the bowl in question, promptly toppled it backwards, thus eliminating any chance it might have stood of reducing the tally.

Before   After

'Nonsense,' said George, in reply to Arnold's angry protestations. 'Falling all the time. . . . As I said, four it is. Well bowled, Ralph.'

Ralph felt uncomfortable. He apologized for the misfortune, but Arnold was not to be mollified. . . . 'If I had known we were playing pairs, I would have brought a partner.'

The perceptive reader will have already spotted one or two grave errors on the part of our chubby hero and, at this point, the aspiring marker is invited to study further examples of his various misdemeanours – and to memorize the following Code of Conduct, in preparation for a written test.

MARKERS

Code of Conduct

DOs

1. Maintain strict impartiality, and extend equal courtesies to both participants. (Even if marking for next of kin.)

2. Measure carefully – a clumsy marker can score more shots than either competitor.

3. Keep a neat and accurate score card. Careless errors may lead to a grave miscarriage of justice, and a spate of acrimonious recriminations.

4. Answer the particular question that is asked – and nothing else. Avoid lengthy rigmaroles regarding possibilities or probabilities. If you are not certain, say so.

5. Pay attention – and be on hand to answer queries.

6. Make sure you know which bowls are whose. Competitor under the impression that he holds the shot may decide not to bowl the last wood. Should he subsequently discover that he is 2 down, he has a legitimate grievance.

7. When not answering questions, keep away from the head. Retire to corner of the rink and keep still.

DON'Ts

1. Do not, in order to cut down your walking, attempt to influence the length of jack. Avoid show of annoyance if competitor fails to deliver jack to your feet.

2. Do not decide that jack is 'not up' without giving competitors the chance to reach agreement by discussion, or having it measured.

3. Do not offer tactical advice on which hand to play, or which shot to attempt.

4. Do not display your contempt – even if the standard of bowling does not come up to your expectations.

5. Do not use the occasion to illustrate your extensive knowledge of the Laws of the Game.

6. Do not, under any circumstances, offer uninvited comments, or take a fiendish delight in the hopeless plight of a luckless competitor.

   Gleeful cries of: 'You're in a spot of bother here' or 'My word, you'll need a good one this time' are unhelpful to the player about to deliver his last bowl.

On reaching the end of this chapter, readers are invited to assess their own marking potential by noting down – from memory – as many points as they can recall from the Code of Conduct, and the more disturbing excerpts from the Ralph *v.* Arnold match.

Candidates are on their honour to mark their own papers, and to make an objective assessment of their future worth by referring to the following table.

MARKING APTITUDE TEST
Assessment Table

Score	Comment	Remarks
15+	Very good	Too good. Try and make a few mistakes, or advertise your woods in the local paper. Your services will be in such demand that you will rarely get the chance of a game.
11–14	Good	County Competition standard. You may look forward to a career spiced with free drinks, free travel and a selection of choice delicacies from competitors' gardens.
6–10	Fair	Perfectly adequate for general club purposes.

Pass
_____

Fail

2–5	Poor	Mark only for your very best friends and close relatives.
1	Very poor	Mark only for members you dislike intensely.
0	See me	Congratulations. Don't bother to buy a measure.

Meanwhile, back on Rink 4, the atmosphere had become decidedly frigid. Ralph was embarrassed; Arnold was incensed; and the marker was chalking up a sound 0/15.

'One to Arnold,' said George, as the end was concluded. 'Eight to fourteen.'

'Eight what?' yelped Arnold. Having been 4 down before winning the last three ends, he was distressed to learn that he was now 6 down. 'Give me that.' He snatched the score card from our hero's podgy fingers, and the sight that he beheld provoked a strangled oath.

Ralph's timely intervention prevented Arnold from pursuing a course of action which he might have afterwards regretted, and the dispute was amicably settled by starting another card with the correct score of 13–12 to Arnold, and relieving the marker of any further responsibility in the matter.

We shall not distress our reader by dwelling in detail on the whole of the game. Suffice it to say that George, although momentarily subdued by his dismissal from the post of official scorer, was by no means a spent force – he was merely biding his time.

Taking advantage of this welcome lull, the players settled down to a good line and length, and the game took on an air of conventional normality which, quite frankly, George found somewhat tedious. He resolved that it was high time to reassert his ascendancy by introducing a selection of the finer points of the marker's craft, in order to provide the game with a greater degree of spectator appeal.

In support of his averred intention of raising the standard of marking, he had rummaged in the dusty cupboards of the clubhouse to unearth a comprehensive array of equipment, comprising; one 100ft tape measure; three sets of callipers; a long string measure; two sets of feeler gauges and a motley collection of wedges of various shapes and sizes. And, come what may, he was jolly well going to use them.

As a modest beginning – brushing aside the pleas of the satisfied competitors, and the handicap of an ancient tape rusted in its spool – a whole series of jacks were queried and measured.

The fact that, on every occasion, they proved to be at least three yards over the limit did nothing to weaken his resolve.

Bowls that showed no sign of toppling over were carefully wedged.

Shots that had been willingly conceded were scrutinized with callipers and feeler gauges.

And endless time was wasted manipulating the long string measure on a wood that was later identified as a stray from the adjoining rink.

Arnold looked at his watch. The whole miserable business had now dragged on for almost two hours. His feet were cold and his heart was heavy, particularly at the thought of his shepherd's pie, by now almost certainly on the hot plate and steadily assuming the consistency of a disused gravel pit.

George, too, was concerned. Time was running out and there was still one aspect of the marker's repertoire which had not yet been included – without which, he considered, no game could lay claim to be regarded as a complete and artistic whole.

The score was 17–16 to Ralph, and he had drawn three excellent bowls. But Arnold had not been found wanting, and it was a close thing. Too exhausted by now to make the trip to see for himself, he foolishly accepted the marker's pronouncement that he was, at the very least, 2 down. Summoning his last reserves of skill and concentration Arnold played a brilliant running bowl and took out the shot wood as clean as a whistle. Elated and flushed with success, he arrived at the head, only to discover that he had neatly removed his own bowl to leave his opponent lying three shots.

'Oh, that was yours, was it?' said George. 'You really ought to get some stickers for your woods, you know.'

Ralph's last bowl trickled into the head to complete a tidy group of four, tightly packed around the jack.

'Oh, well bowled, young man,' cried George. 'Lying game,' he called down the rink. He turned to Arnold, who was staring glumly down at the head, and nudged him with his elbow. 'He's lying game, you know,' he said confidentially.

'I heard,' snarled the unfortunate Arnold, and he stomped irritably back to the mat.

George frowned. He had just realized the full implications of the situation. If Arnold failed with his last wood the game was over, and the opportunity he had been relishing with such pleasurable anticipation would be lost.

'Hmmm. . . .' he murmured, stroking his chin thoughtfully.

On the mat, Arnold stared dejectedly at the tiny knot of woods. He had no option but to fire . . . and he was dead on line. It sped like a homing missile locked on target. But just as it was about to scatter the four woods to the far corners of the green, George pounced.

With a single bound he was in front of the head, snatching up the speeding bowl with the swiftness of a serpent's tongue.

Arnold gasped in amazement. In the window seats the shocked silence was shattered only by the clatter of pipes falling from open mouths. . . .

George raised the bowl aloft in triumph. . . . 'Foot fault!' he cried. 'Game to Ralph.'

'Well played, Ralph,' said George, extending a congratulating hand, 'and commiserations, Arnold.'

'Commiserations be * * * * * *!' said Arnold.

*

It was the first, and indeed, the only time in the history of the Highcliffe BC that a marker had been sacked on the spot.

Ralph, naturally, refused to accept victory on such terms and an ad hoc meeting of committee members present decreed that the game should be replayed, and appointed a new marker for the following evening.

Arnold won fairly easily. It was a good game, but as Old Tom observed, it was somewhat lacking in the thrills and spills and the spectator appeal of the previous evening.

'Congratulations, Arnold. Well played,' said George, as the competitors came to the bar. 'I'll have that pint now. . . .' George prodded him with a stubby finger – perhaps the fellow was a little on deaf side. 'Customary thing, old man,' he prompted. 'You know – for the victor to buy the marker a drink.'

After a moment, George turned to Ralph with furrowed brow: 'What a strange chap,' he said. 'Why did he walk off like that? . . . Someone upset him?'

Epilogue

And so the season drew to a close. The competitions were completed; the trophies awarded – and the first autumn leaves speckled the green and nestled in the ditches.

It was time to pack the bags, empty the lockers and shutter the clubhouse window for the long winter months ahead.

On closing day, after much handshaking and admonitions to 'winter well', the members went their separate ways and our two heroes, heavily laden with bags, hold-alls and the assorted bric-à-brac that the bowler accumulates during the season, paused at the gate for one last look.

Ralph felt a tinge of sadness at the sight of the rickety old clubhouse, desolate and deserted now, snuggling in the glow of a late September evening.

The green, damp with the evening dew, looked empty and forlorn. Only the occasional crinkled leaf, caught up in the soft breeze, bowled and bounced across the ancient turf – now bearing the honourable scars of devoted service to a long and happy season.

Ralph consoled himself with the thought that he would be back again next spring and, like the green, ready for a fresh start – a better and he hoped, a wiser bowler.

They closed the gate behind them and walked in silence for a few moments, crushing the crisp leaves underfoot.

'All goods things come to an end,' said Ralph, not very originally.

'Never mind,' said George. 'Another year – another season. You know, Ralph – I've got the feeling in my bones that we shall really make our mark next season. Now that we've got the hang of things.'

Ralph nodded. He didn't like to mention it, but he couldn't help feeling that George had already contributed more than his fair share of marks.

'Oh, yes,' said George. 'Never look back, you know. No point. . . . Always look to the future, old chap.'

But as they strolled along in companionable silence, it was doubtful whether either of them had the faintest inkling of what that future held in store. . . .

How, before long, they would find themselves elected to the committee, to be acquainted at first hand with that most stimulating of all institutions – the Bowls Club Committee Meeting.

How Ralph was to become a very good player, and meet with great success. Of the gruelling trial by ordeal that he would undergo to win, and wear with pride, his County Badge.

How George – shrewdly assessing that the actual bowling of woods was never to be his strong point – wisely elected to make his mark on the administrative side. Of his meteoric rise to fame – from humble Club Captain to an officer of the County Association – thence to the very highest pinnacles of the bowling world.

And how it came to pass that our heroes' wives, wearying of their roles as bowling widows, finally rebelled and applied for full membership. Of George's mortification at the remarkable natural talent displayed by his good and gentle lady wife. 'It was,' he was heard to observe, 'thoroughly indecent.' Of the inauguration of the Husband and Wife Mixed Pairs Tournament, later abandoned as a result of three estrangements and one decree nisi. Of the ill-fated tour to Budleigh Salterton, and the adventures that befell the little party . . . and the scandalous affair of the . . .

but that's another story.